Optional Protocol 2

The titles published in this series are listed at *brill.com/cunc*

A Commentary on the United Nations Convention
on the Rights of the Child

Editors

Ton Liefaard and Julia Sloth-Nielsen

Optional Protocol 2

*On the Sale of Children, Child Prostitution
and Child Pornography*

By

Sabine K. Witting

Assistant Professor at Leiden University, eLaw—Center for Law and Digital Technologies

BRILL
NIJHOFF

LEIDEN | BOSTON
2022

Cover illustration by Nadia, 1½ years old.

The Library of Congress Cataloging-in-Publication Data is available online at https://catalog.loc.gov
LC record available at https://lccn.loc.gov/2022046347

Cite as: Sabine K. Witting, "Optional Protocol: On the Sale of Children, Child Prostitution and Child Pornography", in: Jaap Doek, Mariëlle Bruning and Benyam Mezmur (Eds.) *A Commentary on the United Nations Convention on the Rights of the Child* (Brill Nijhoff Publishers, Leiden, 2022).

ISSN 1574-8626
ISBN 978-90-04-46450-6 (paperback)
ISBN 978-90-04-46039-3 (e-book)

CONTENTS

ABBREVIATIONS

ACERWC	African Committee of Experts on the Rights and Welfare of the Child
ACRWC	African Charter on the Rights and Welfare of the Child
COVID-19	Coronavirus Disease 2019
CRC	UN Convention on the Rights of the Child
CRC Committee	Committee on the Rights of the Child
CSAM	Child sexual abuse material
ECPAT	Every Child Protected Against Trafficking
EU	European Union
ICMEC	International Centre for Missing and Exploited Children
ICT	Information and Communication Technologies
ILO	International Labour Organisation
INTERPOL	International Criminal Police Organisation
ITU	International Telecommunication Union
IWF	Internet Watch Foundation
LGBTIQ	Lesbian, gay, bisexual, transsexual, intersexual and queer
LOIPR	List of Issues Prior to Reporting
MLA	Mutual Legal Assistance
NGO	Non-governmental organisation
OPSC	Optional Protocol on the sale of children, child prostitution and child pornography
SECTT	Sexual Exploitation of Children in Travel and Tourism
UN	United Nations
UNICEF	United Nations Children's Fund
UNODC	United Nations Office for Drugs and Crime

AUTHOR BIOGRAPHY

Dr. Sabine K. Witting is an Assistant Professor at Leiden University, Center for Law and Digital Technologies (eLaw). She studied Law at Goethe University Frankfurt am Main and China University of Political Science and Law and holds a PhD from Leiden University titled 'Child sexual abuse in the digital era—Rethinking legal frameworks and transnational law enforcement collaboration'.

Her research and teaching focuses on the regulation, investigation and prosecution of online child sexual abuse, cyber trafficking and image-based sexual assault, gender-sensitive and child-friendly access to justice in (online) sexual violence cases and balancing right to protection from sexual abuse and exploitation, rule of law and right to privacy and data protection in the digital space.

Since 2015, Dr. Witting has been working for the United Nations in Eastern and Southern Africa, Southeast Asia and the Pacific region. In this role, she advises Governments, regional bodies, civil society and other stakeholders on prevention and response to (online) violence against women and children, legal reform and access to justice.

ACKNOWLEDGMENTS

I would like to thank Prof Ton Liefaard and Prof Julia Sloth-Nielsen for entrusting me with this important contribution to the CRC Commentary series and for their unwavering support throughout the conceptualisation and development process. Further, I would like to express my sincere gratitude to Prof Jaap Doek for his thorough review of this OPSC commentary and for offering his unmatchable technical expertise to make this commentary what it is today.

OPTIONAL PROTOCOL TO THE CONVENTION ON THE RIGHTS OF THE CHILD ON THE SALE OF CHILDREN, CHILD PROSTITUTION AND CHILD PORNOGRAPHY

The States Parties to the present Protocol,

Considering that, in order further to achieve the purposes of the Convention on the Rights of the Child and the implementation of its provisions, especially articles 1, 11, 21, 32, 33, 34, 35 and 36, it would be appropriate to extend the measures that States Parties should undertake in order to guarantee the protection of the child from the sale of children, child prostitution and child pornography,

Considering also that the Convention on the Rights of the Child recognizes the right of the child to be protected from economic exploitation and from performing any work that is likely to be hazardous or to interfere with the child's education, or to be harmful to the child's health or physical, mental, spiritual, moral or social development,

Gravely concerned at the significant and increasing international traffic of children for the purpose of the sale of children, child prostitution and child pornography,

Les États Parties au présent Protocole,

Considérant que, pour aller de l'avant dans la réalisation des buts de la Convention relative aux droits de l'enfant et l'application de ses dispositions, en particulier des articles premier, 11, 21, 32, 33, 34, 35 et 36, il serait approprié d'élargir les mesures que les États Parties devraient prendre pour garantir la protection de l'enfant contre la vente d'enfants, la prostitution des enfants et la pornographie mettant en scène des enfants,

Considérant également que la Convention relative aux droits de l'enfant consacre le droit de l'enfant d'être protégé contre l'exploitation économique et de ne pas être astreint à un travail comportant des risques ou susceptible de compromettre son éducation ou de nuire à sa santé ou à son développement physique, mental, spirituel, moral ou social,

Constatant avec une vive préoccupation que la traite internationale d'enfants aux fins de la vente d'enfants, de la prostitution des enfants et de la pornographie mettant en scène des enfants revêt

Deeply concerned at the widespread and continuing practice of sex tourism, to which children are especially vulnerable, as it directly promotes the sale of children, child prostitution and child pornography,

Recognizing that a number of particularly vulnerable groups, including girl children, are at greater risk of sexual exploitation, and that girl children are disproportionately represented among the sexually exploited,

Concerned about the growing availability of child pornography on the Internet and other evolving technologies, and recalling the International Conference on Combating Child Pornography on the Internet (Vienna, 1999) and, in particular, its conclusion calling for the worldwide criminalization of the production, distribution, exportation, transmission, importation, intentional possession and advertising of child pornography, and stressing the importance of closer cooperation and partnership between Governments and the Internet industry,

des proportions considérables et croissantes,

Profondément préoccupés par la pratique répandue et persistante du tourisme sexuel auquel les enfants sont particulièrement exposés, dans la mesure où il favorise directement la vente d'enfants, la prostitution des enfants et la pornographie mettant en scène des enfants,

Conscients qu'un certain nombre de groupes particulièrement vulnérables, notamment les fillettes, sont davantage exposés au risque d'exploitation sexuelle, et que l'on recense un nombre anormalement élevé de fillettes parmi les victimes de l'exploitation sexuelle,

Préoccupés par l'offre croissante de matériels pornographiques mettant en scène des enfants sur l'Internet et autres nouveaux supports technologiques, et rappelant que, dans ses conclusions, la Conférence internationale sur la lutte contre la pornographie impliquant des enfants sur l'Internet, tenue à Vienne en 1999, a notamment demandé la criminalisation dans le monde entier de la production, la distribution, l'exportation, l'importation, la transmission, la possession intentionnelle et la publicité de matériels pornographiques impliquant des enfants, et soulignant l'importance d'une coopération et d'un partenariat plus étroits entre les

Believing that the elimination of the sale of children, child prostitution and child pornography will be facilitated by adopting a holistic approach, addressing the contributing factors, including underdevelopment, poverty, economic disparities, inequitable socio-economic structure, dysfunctioning families, lack of education, urban-rural migration, gender discrimination, irresponsible adult sexual behaviour, harmful traditional practices, armed conflicts and trafficking of children,

Believing that efforts to raise public awareness are needed to reduce consumer demand for the sale of children, child prostitution and child pornography, and also believing in the importance of strengthening global partnership among all actors and of improving law enforcement at the national level,

Noting the provisions of international legal instruments relevant to the protection of children, including the Hague Convention on the Protection of Children and Cooperation with Respect to Inter-Country Adoption, the Hague Convention on the Civil

pouvoirs publics et les professionnels de l'Internet,

Convaincus que l'élimination de la vente d'enfants, de la prostitution des enfants et de la pornographie mettant en scène des enfants sera facilitée par l'adoption d'une approche globale tenant compte des facteurs qui contribuent à ces phénomènes, notamment le sous-développement, la pauvreté, les disparités économiques, l'inéquité des structures socioéconomiques, les dysfonctionnements familiaux, le manque d'éducation, l'exode rural, la discrimination fondée sur le sexe, le comportement sexuel irresponsable des adultes, les pratiques traditionnelles préjudiciables, les conflits armés et la traite des enfants,

Estimant qu'une action de sensibilisation du public est nécessaire pour réduire la demande qui est à l'origine de la vente d'enfants, de la prostitution des enfants et de la pornographie pédophile, et qu'il importe de renforcer le partenariat mondial entre tous les acteurs et d'améliorer l'application de la loi au niveau national,

Prenant note des dispositions des instruments juridiques internationaux pertinents en matière de protection des enfants, notamment la Convention de La Haye sur la protection des enfants et la coopération en matière d'adoption

Aspects of International Child Abduction, the Hague Convention on Jurisdiction, Applicable Law, Recognition, Enforcement and Cooperation in Respect of Parental Responsibility and Measures for the Protection of Children, and International Labour Organization Convention No. 182 on the Prohibition and Immediate Action for the Elimination of the Worst Forms of Child Labour,

Encouraged by the overwhelming support for the Convention on the Rights of the Child, demonstrating the widespread commitment that exists for the promotion and protection of the rights of the child,

Recognizing the importance of the implementation of the provisions of the Programme of Action for the Prevention of the Sale of Children, Child Prostitution and Child Pornography and the Declaration and Agenda for Action adopted at the World Congress against Commercial Sexual Exploitation of Children, held at Stockholm from 27 to 31 August 1996, and the other relevant decisions and recommendations of pertinent international bodies,

Taking due account of the importance of the traditions and cultural values of each people for the protection

internationale, la Convention de La Haye sur les aspects civils de l'enlèvement international d'enfants, la Convention de La Haye concernant la compétence, la loi applicable, la reconnaissance, l'exécution et la coopération en matière de responsabilité parentale et de mesures de protection des enfants, et la Convention no 182 de l'Organisation internationale du Travail concernant l'interdiction des pires formes de travail des enfants et l'action immédiate en vue de leur élimination,

Encouragés par l'appui considérable recueilli par la Convention relative aux droits de l'enfant, qui dénote une volonté générale de promouvoir et de protéger les droits de l'enfant,

Considérant qu'il importe de mettre en œuvre les dispositions du Programme d'action pour la prévention de la vente d'enfants, de la prostitution des enfants et de la pornographie impliquant des enfants et de la Déclaration et du Programme d'action adoptés en 1996 au Congrès mondial contre l'exploitation sexuelle des enfants à des fins commerciales, tenu à Stockholm du 27 au 31 août 1996, ainsi que les autres décisions et recommandations pertinentes des organismes internationaux concernés,

Tenant dûment compte de l'importance des traditions et des valeurs culturelles de chaque peuple

and harmonious development of the child,

Have agreed as follows:

Article 1

States Parties shall prohibit the sale of children, child prostitution and child pornography as provided for by the present Protocol.

Article 2

For the purpose of the present Protocol:

> (a) Sale of children means any act or transaction whereby a child is transferred by any person or group of persons to another for remuneration or any other consideration;

> (b) Child prostitution means the use of a child in sexual activities for remuneration or any other form of consideration;

> (c) Child pornography means any representation, by whatever means, of a child engaged in real or simulated explicit sexual activities or any representation of the sexual parts of a child for primarily sexual purposes.

pour la protection de l'enfant et son développement harmonieux,

Sont convenus de ce qui suit:

Article premier

Les États Parties interdisent la vente d'enfants, la prostitution des enfants et la pornographie mettant en scène des enfants conformément aux dispositions du présent Protocole.

Article 2

Aux fins du présent Protocole:

> a) On entend par vente d'enfants tout acte ou toute transaction en vertu desquels un enfant es remis par toute personne ou de tout groupe de personnes à une autre personne ou un autre groupe contre rémunération ou tout autre avantage;

> b) On entend par prostitution des enfants le fait d'utiliser un enfant aux fins d'activités sexuelles contre rémunération ou toute autre forme d'avantage;

> c) On entend par pornographie mettant en scène des enfants toute représentation, par quelque moyen que ce soit, d'un enfant s'adonnant à des activités sexuelles explicites, réelles ou simulées, ou toute représentation des organes sexuels d'un enfant, à des fins principalement sexuelles.

Article 3

1. Each State Party shall ensure that, as a minimum, the following acts and activities are fully covered under its criminal or penal law, whether these offences are committed domestically or transnationally or on an individual or organized basis:

    (a) In the context of sale of children as defined in Article 2:

      (i) The offering, delivering or accepting, by whatever means, a child for the purpose of:

        a. Sexual exploitation of the child;

        b. Transfer of organs of the child for profit;

        c. Engagement of the child in forced labour;

      (ii) Improperly inducing consent, as an intermediary, for the adoption of a child in violation of applicable international legal instruments on adoption;

    (b) Offering, obtaining, procuring or providing a child for child prostitution, as defined in Article 2;

    (c) Producing, distributing, disseminating, importing, exporting, offering,

Article 3

1. Chaque État Partie veille à ce que, au minimum, les actes et activités suivants soient pleinement couverts par son droit pénal, que ces infractions soient commises au plan interne ou transnational, par un individu ou de façon organisée:

    a) Dans le cadre de la vente d'enfants telle que définie à l'article 2:

      i) Le fait d'offrir, de remettre, ou d'accepter un enfant, quel que soit le moyen utilisé, aux fins:

        a. D'éxploitation sexuelle de l'enfant;

        b. De transfert d'organe de l'enfant à titre onéreux;

        c. De soumettre l'enfant au travail forcé;

      ii) Le fait d'obtenir indûment, en tant qu'intermédiaire, le consentement à l'adoption d'un enfant, en violation des instruments juridiques internationaux relatifs à l'adoption;

    b) Le fait d'offrir, d'obtenir, de procurer ou de fournir un enfant à des fins de prostitution, telle que définie à l'article 2;

    c) Le fait de produire, de distribuer, de diffuser, d'importer, d'exporter,

selling or possessing for the above purposes child pornography as defined in Article 2.

2. Subject to the provisions of a State Party's national law, the same shall apply to an attempt to commit any of these acts and to complicity or participation in any of these acts.

3. Each State Party shall make these offences punishable by appropriate penalties that take into account their grave nature.

4. Subject to the provisions of its national law, each State Party shall take measures, where appropriate, to establish the liability of legal persons for offences established in paragraph I of the present Article. Subject to the legal principles of the State Party, this liability of legal persons may be criminal, civil or administrative.

5. States Parties shall take all appropriate legal and administrative measures to ensure that all persons involved in the adoption of a child act in conformity with applicable international legal instruments.

d'offrir, de vendre ou de détenir aux fins susmentionnées, des matériels pornographiques mettant en scène des enfants, tels que définis à l'article 2.

2. Sous réserve du droit interne d'un État Partie, les mêmes dispositions valent en cas de tentative de commission de l'un quelconque de ces actes, de complicité dans sa commission ou de participation à celle-ci.

3. Tout État Partie rend ces infractions passibles de peines appropriées tenant compte de leur gravité.

4. Sous réserve des dispositions de son droit interne, tout État Partie prend, s'il y a lieu, les mesures qui s'imposent, afin d'établir la responsabilité des personnes morales pour les infractions visées au paragraphe 1 du présent article. Selon les principes juridiques de l'État Partie, cette responsabilité peut être pénale, civile ou administrative.

5. Les États Parties prennent toutes les mesures juridiques et administratives appropriées pour s'assurer que toutes les personnes intervenant dans l'adoption d'un enfant agissent conformément aux dispositions des instruments juridiques internationaux applicables.

Article 4

1. Each State Party shall take such measures as may be necessary to establish its jurisdiction over the offences referred to in Article 3, paragraph 1, when the offences are committed in its territory or on board a ship or aircraft registered in that State.

2. Each State Party may take such measures as may be necessary to establish its jurisdiction over the offences referred to in Article 3, paragraph 1, in the following cases:
   (a) When the alleged offender is a national of that State or a person who has his habitual residence in its territory;
   (b) When the victim is a national of that State.

3. Each State Party shall also take such measures as may be necessary to establish its jurisdiction over the above-mentioned offences when the alleged offender is present in its territory and it does not extradite him or her to another State Party on the ground that the offence has been committed by one of its nationals.

4. This Protocol does not exclude any criminal jurisdiction exercised in accordance with internal law.

Article 4

1. Tout État Partie prend les mesures nécessaires pour établir sa compétence aux fins de connaître des infractions visées au paragraphe 1 de l'article 3, lorsque ces infractions ont été commises sur son territoire ou à bord de navires ou d'aéronefs immatriculés dans cet État.

2. Tout État Partie peut prendre les mesures nécessaires pour établir sa compétence aux fins de connaître des infractions visées au paragraphe 1 de l'article 3, dans les cas suivants:
   a) Lorsque l'auteur présumé de l'infraction est un ressortissant dudit État, ou a sa résidence habituelle sur le territoire de celui-ci;
   b) Lorsque la victime est un ressortissant dudit État.

3. Tout État Partie prend également les mesures propres à établir sa compétence aux fins de connaître des infractions susmentionnées lorsque l'auteur présumé de l'infraction est présent sur son territoire et qu'il ne l'extrade pas vers un autre État Partie au motif que l'infraction a été commise par l'un de ses ressortissants.

4. Le présent Protocole n'exclut aucune compétence pénale exercée conformément aux lois nationales.

Article 5	Article 5
1. The offences referred to in Article 3, paragraph 1, shall be deemed to be included as extraditable offences in any extradition treaty existing between States Parties and shall be included as extraditable offences in every extradition treaty subsequently concluded between them, in accordance with the conditions set forth in those treaties.	1. Les infractions visées au paragraphe 1 de l'article 3 sont de plein droit comprises dans tout traité d'extradition en vigueur entre les États Parties et sont comprises dans tout traité d'extradition qui sera conclu ultérieurement entre eux, conformément aux conditions énoncées dans lesdits traités.
2. If a State Party that makes extradition conditional on the existence of a treaty receives a request for extradition from another State Party with which it has no extradition treaty, it may consider this Protocol as a legal basis for extradition in respect of such offences. Extradition shall be subject to the conditions provided by the law of the requested State.	2. Si un État Partie qui subordonne l'extradition à l'existence d'un traité est saisi d'une demande d'extradition par un autre État Partie avec lequel il n'est pas lié par un traité d'extradition, il peut considérer le présent Protocole comme constituant la base juridique de l'extradition en ce qui concerne lesdites infractions. L'extradition est subordonnée aux conditions prévues par le droit de l'État requis.
3. States Parties that do not make extradition conditional on the existence of a treaty shall recognize such offences as extraditable offences between themselves subject to the conditions provided by the law of the requested State.	3. Les États Parties qui ne subordonnent pas l'extradition à l'existence d'un traité reconnaissent lesdites infractions comme cas d'extradition entre eux dans les conditions prévues par le droit de l'État requis.
4. Such offences shall be treated, for the purpose of extradition between States Parties, as if they had been committed not only in	4. Entre États Parties, lesdites infractions sont considérées aux fins d'extradition comme ayant été commises non seulement au

the place in which they occurred but also in the territories of the States required to establish their jurisdiction in accordance with Article 4.

5. If an extradition request is made with respect to an offence described in Article 3, paragraph 1, and if the requested State Party does not or will not extradite on the basis of the nationality of the offender, that State shall take suitable measures to submit the case to its competent authorities for the purpose of prosecution.

Article 6

1. States Parties shall afford one another the greatest measure of assistance in connection with investigations or criminal or extradition proceedings brought in respect of the offences set forth in Article 3, paragraph 1, including assistance in obtaining evidence at their disposal necessary for the proceedings.

2. States Parties shall carry out their obligations under paragraph 1 of the present Article in conformity with any treaties or other arrangements on mutual legal assistance that may exist between them. In the absence of such treaties or arrangements, States Parties shall afford one another

lieu de leur perpétration, mais aussi sur le territoire placé sous la juridiction des États tenus d'établir leur compétence en vertu de l'article 4.

5. Si une demande d'extradition est présentée au motif d'une infraction visée au paragraphe 1 de l'article 3, et si l'État requis n'extrade pas ou ne veut pas extrader, à raison de la nationalité de l'auteur de l'infraction, cet État prend les mesures voulues pour saisir ses autorités compétentes aux fins de poursuites.

Article 6

1. Les États Parties s'accordent l'entraide la plus large possible pour toute enquête, procédure pénale ou procédure d'extradition relative aux infractions visées au paragraphe 1 de l'article 3, y compris pour l'obtention des éléments de preuve dont ils disposent et qui sont nécessaires aux fins de la procédure.

2. Les États Parties s'acquittent de leurs obligations en vertu du paragraphe 1 du présent article en conformité avec tout traité ou accord d'entraide judiciaire qui peut exister entre eux. En l'absence d'un tel traité ou accord, les États Parties s'accordent cette entraide

assistance in accordance with their domestic law.

Article 7

States Parties shall, subject to the provisions of their national law:
(a) Take measures to provide for the seizure and confiscation, as appropriate, of:

(i) Goods such as materials, assets and other instrumentalities used to commit or facilitate offences under the present Protocol;

(ii) Proceeds derived from such offences;
(b) Execute requests from another State Party for seizure or confiscation of goods or proceeds referred to in subparagraph (a) (i);
(c) Take measures aimed at closing, on a temporary or definitive basis, premises used to commit such offences.

Article 8

1. States Parties shall adopt appropriate measures to protect the rights and interests of child victims of the practices prohibited under the present Protocol at all stages of the criminal justice process, in particular by:

conformément à leur droit interne.

Article 7

Sous réserve des dispositions de leur droit interne, les États Parties:
a) Prennent des mesures appropriées pour permettre la saisie et la confiscation, selon que de besoin:

i) Des biens tels que documents, avoirs et autres moyens matériels utilisés pour commettre les infractions visées dans le présent Protocole ou en faciliter la commission;

ii) Du produit de ces infractions;

b) Donnent effet aux demandes de saisie ou de confiscation des biens ou produits visés auxparagraphe a) émanant d'un autre État Partie;

c) Prennent des mesures en vue de fermer provisoirement ou définitivement les locaux utilisés pour commettre lesdites infractions.

Article 8

1. Les États Parties adoptent à tous les stades de la procédure pénale les mesures nécessaires pour protéger les droits et les intérêts des enfants victimes des pratiques proscrites par le présent Protocole, en particulier:

(a) Recognizing the vulnerability of child victims and adapting procedures to recognize their special needs, including their special needs as witnesses;

(b) Informing child victims of their rights, their role and the scope, timing and progress of the proceedings and of the disposition of their cases;

(c) Allowing the views, needs and concerns of child victims to be presented and considered in proceedings where their personal interests are affected, in a mariner consistent with the procedural rules of national law;

(d) Providing appropriate support services to child victims throughout the legal process;

(e) Protecting, as appropriate, the privacy and identity of child victims and taking measures in accordance with national law to avoid the inappropriate dissemination of information that could

a) En reconnaissant la vulnérabilité des enfants victimes et en adaptant les procédures de manière à tenir compte de leurs besoins particuliers, notamment en tant que témoins;

b) En tenant les enfants victimes informés de leurs droits, de leur rôle ainsi que de la portée, du calendrier et du déroulement de la procédure, et de la décision rendue dans leur affaire;

c) En permettant que les vues, les besoins ou les préoccupations des enfants victimes soient présentés et examinés au cours de la procédure lorsque leurs intérêts personnels sont en jeu, d'une manière conforme aux règles de procédure du droit interne;

d) En fournissant une assistance appropriée aux enfants victimes à tous les stades de la procédure judiciaire;

e) En protégeant, s'il y a lieu, la vie privée et l'identité des enfants victimes et en prenant des mesures conformes au droit interne pour prévenir la diffusion de toute information

lead to the identification of child victims;

(f) Providing, in appropriate cases, for the safety of child victims, as well as that of their families and witnesses on their behalf, from intimidation and retaliation;

(g) Avoiding unnecessary delay in the disposition of cases and the execution of orders or decrees granting compensation to child victims.

2. States Parties shall ensure that uncertainty as to the actual age of the victim shall not prevent the initiation of criminal investigations, including investigations aimed at establishing the age of the victim.

3. States Parties shall ensure that, in the treatment by the criminal justice system of children who are victims of the offences described in the present Protocol, the best interest of the child shall be a primary consideration.

4. States Parties shall take measures to ensure appropriate training, in particular legal and psychological training, for the persons who work with victims of the offences prohibited under the present Protocol.

pouvant conduire à leur identification;

f) En veillant, le cas échéant, à ce que les enfants victimes, ainsi que leur famille et les témoins à charge, soient à l'abri de l'intimidation et des représailles;

g) En évitant tout retard indu dans le prononcé du jugement et l'exécution des ordonnances ou des décisions accordant une indemnisation aux enfants victimes.

2. Les États Parties veillent à ce qu'une incertitude quant à l'âge réel de la victime n'empêche pas l'ouverture d'enquêtes pénales, notamment d'enquêtes visant à déterminer cet âge.

3. Les États Parties veillent à ce que, dans la manière dont le système de justice pénale traite les enfants victimes des infractions décrites dans le présent Protocole, l'intérêt supérieur de l'enfant soit la considération première.

4. Les États Parties prennent des mesures pour dispenser une formation appropriée, en particulier dans les domaines juridique et psychologique, aux personnes qui s'occupent des

5.   States Parties shall, in appropriate cases, adopt measures in order to protect the safety and integrity of those persons and/or organizations involved in the prevention and/or protection and rehabilitation of victims of such offences.

6.   Nothing in the present Article shall be construed as prejudicial to or inconsistent with the rights of the accused to a fair and impartial trial.

Article 9

1.   States Parties shall adopt or strengthen, implement and disseminate laws, administrative measures, social policies and programmes to prevent the offences referred to in the present Protocol. Particular attention shall be given to protect children who are especially vulnerable to these practices.

2.   States Parties shall promote awareness in the public at large, including children, through information by all appropriate means, education and training, about the preventive measures and harmful effects of the offences referred to in the present Protocol. In fulfilling their obligations under this Article, States Parties shall

victimes des infractions visées dans le présent Protocole.

5.   S'il y a lieu, les États Parties font le nécessaire pour garantir la sécurité et l'intégrité des personnes et/ou des organismes de prévention et/ou de protection et de réadaptation des victimes de telles infractions.

6.   Aucune des dispositions du présent article ne porte atteinte au droit de l'accusé à un procès équitable et impartial ou n'est incompatible avec ce droit.

Article 9

1.   Les États Parties adoptent ou renforcent, appliquent et diffusent des lois, mesures administratives, politiques et programmes sociaux pour prévenir les infractions visées dans le présent Protocole. Une attention spéciale est accordée à la protection des enfants particulièrement exposés à de telles pratiques.

2.   Par l'information à l'aide de tous les moyens appropriés, l'éducation et la formation, les États Parties sensibilisent le grand public, y compris les enfants, aux mesures propres à prévenir les pratiques proscrites par le présent Protocole et aux effets néfastes de ces dernières. Pour s'acquitter de leurs obligations en vertu du

encourage the participation of the community and, in particular, children and child victims, in such information and education and training programmes, including at the international level.

3. States Parties shall take all feasible measures with the aim of ensuring all appropriate assistance to victims of such offences, including their full social reintegration and their full physical and psychological recovery.

4. States Parties shall ensure that all child victims of the offences described in the present Protocol have access to adequate procedures to seek, without discrimination, compensation for damages from those legally responsible.

5. States Parties shall take appropriate measures aimed at effectively prohibiting the production and dissemination of material advertising the offences described in the present Protocol.

Article 10
1. States Parties shall take all necessary steps to strengthen international cooperation by multilateral, regional and

présent article, les États Parties encouragent la participation des communautés et, en particulier, des enfants et des enfants victimes, à ces programmes d'information, d'éducation et de formation, y compris au niveau international.

3. Les États Parties prennent toutes les mesures possibles pour assurer toute l'assistance appropriée aux victimes des infractions visées dans le présent Protocole, notamment leur pleine réinsertion sociale et leur plein rétablissement physique et psychologique.

4. Les États Parties veillent à ce que tous les enfants victimes des infractions décrites dans le présent Protocole aient accès à des procédures leur permettant, sans discrimination, de réclamer réparation du préjudice subi aux personnes juridiquement responsables.

5. Les États Parties prennent des mesures appropriées pour interdire efficacement la production et la diffusion de matériels qui font la publicité des pratiques proscrites dans le présent Protocole.

Article 10
1. Les États Parties prennent toutes les mesures nécessaires pour renforcer la coopération internationale par des accords

bilateral arrangements for the prevention, detection, investigation, prosecution and punishment of those responsible for acts involving the sale of children, child prostitution, child pornography and child sex tourism. States Parties shall also promote international cooperation and coordination between their authorities, national and international non-governmental organizations and international organizations.

2. States Parties shall promote international cooperation to assist child victims in their physical and psychological recovery, social reintegration and repatriation.

3. States Parties shall promote the strengthening of international cooperation in order to address the root causes, such as poverty and underdevelopment, contributing to the vulnerability of children to the sale of children, child prostitution, child pornography and child sex tourism.

4. States Parties in a position to do so shall provide financial, technical or other assistance through existing multilateral, regional, bilateral or other programmes.

multilatéraux, régionaux et bilatéraux ayant pour objet de prévenir, identifier, poursuivre et punir les responsables d'actes liés à la vente d'enfants, à la prostitution des enfants, à la pornographie et au tourisme pédophiles, ainsi que d'enquêter sur de tels actes. Les États Parties favorisent également la coopération et la coordination internationales entre leurs autorités, les organisations non gouvernementales nationales et internationales et les organisations internationales.

2. Les États Parties encouragent la coopération internationale pour aider à la réadaptation physique et psychologique des enfants victimes, à leur réinsertion sociale et à leur rapatriement.

3. Les États Parties s'attachent à renforcer la coopération internationale pour éliminer les principaux facteurs, notamment la pauvreté et le sous-développement, qui rendent les enfants vulnérables à la vente, à la prostitution, à la pornographie et au tourisme pédophiles.

4. Les États Parties qui sont en mesure de le faire fournissent une aide financière, technique ou autre dans le cadre des programmes existants, multilatéraux, régionaux, bilatéraux ou autres.

Article 11

Nothing in the present Protocol shall affect any provisions that are more conducive to the realization of the rights of the child and that may be contained in:

    (a) The law of a State Party;

    (b) International law in force for that State.

Article 12

1. Each State Party shall submit, within two years following the entry into force of the Protocol for that State Party, a report to the Committee on the Rights of the Child providing comprehensive information on the measures it has taken to implement the provisions of the Protocol.

2. Following the submission of the comprehensive report, each State Party shall include in the reports they submit to the Committee on the Rights of the Child, in accordance with Article 44 of the Convention, any further information with respect to the implementation of the Protocol. Other States Parties to the Protocol shall submit a report every five years.

3. The Committee on the Rights of the Child may request from States Parties further information relevant to the implementation of this Protocol.

Article 11

Aucune des dispositions du présent Protocole ne porte atteinte aux dispositions plus propices à la réalisation des droits de l'enfant qui peuvent figurer:

    a) Dans la législation d'un État Partie;

    b) Dans le droit international en vigueur pour cet État.

Article 12

1. Chaque État Partie présente, dans les deux ans à compter de l'entrée en vigueur du présent Protocole à son égard, un rapport au Comité des droits de l'enfant contenant des renseignements détaillés sur les mesures qu'il a prises pour donner effet aux dispositions du Protocole.

2. Après la présentation de son rapport détaillé, chaque État Partie inclut dans les rapports qu'il présente au Comité des droits de l'enfant, conformément à l'article 44 de la Convention, tout complément d'information concernant l'application du présent Protocole. Les autres États Parties au Protocole présentent un rapport tous les cinq ans.

3. Le Comité des droits de l'enfant peut demander aux États Parties un complément d'information concernant l'application du présent Protocole.

Article 13

1. The present Protocol is open for signature by any State that is a party to the Convention or has signed it.

2. The present Protocol is subject to ratification and is open to accession by any State that is a party to the Convention or has signed it. Instruments of ratification or accession shall be deposited with the Secretary-General of the United Nations.

Article 14

1. The present Protocol shall enter into force three months after the deposit of the tenth instrument of ratification or accession.

2. For each State ratifying the present Protocol or acceding to it after its entry into force, the present Protocol shall enter into force one month after the date of the deposit of its own instrument of ratification or accession.

Article 15

1. Any State Party may denounce the present Protocol at any time by written notification to the Secretary-General of the United Nations, who shall thereafter inform the other States Parties to the Convention and all States that have signed the Convention. The denunciation shall I take effect one year after the date of receipt of the notification by the

Article 13

1. Le présent Protocole est ouvert à la signature de tout État qui est Partie à la Convention ou qui l'a signée.

2. Le présent Protocole est soumis à la ratification et est ouvert à l'adhésion de tout État qui est Partie à la Convention ou qui l'a signée. Les instruments de ratification ou d'adhésion seront déposés auprès du Secrétaire général de l'Organisation des Nations Unies.

Article 14

1. Le présent Protocole entrera en vigueur trois mois après la date du dépôt du dixième instrument de ratification ou d'adhésion.

2. Pour chacun des États qui ratifieront le présent Protocole ou y adhéreront après son entrée en vigueur, le Protocole entrera en vigueur un mois après la date du dépôt par cet État de son instrument de ratification ou d'adhésion.

Article 15

1. Tout État Partie peut, à tout moment, dénoncer le présent Protocole par notification écrite adressée au Secrétaire général de l'Organisation des Nations Unies, qui en informe les autres États Parties à la Convention et tous les États qui l'ont signée. La dénonciation prend effet un an après la date à laquelle la

Secretary-General of the United Nations.

2. Such a denunciation shall not have the effect of releasing the State Party from its obligations under this Protocol in regard to any offence that occurs prior to the date on which the denunciation becomes effective. Nor shall such a denunciation prejudice in any way the continued consideration of any matter that is already under consideration by the Committee prior to the date on which the denunciation becomes effective.

Article 16

1. Any State Party may propose an amendment and file it with the Secretary-General of the United Nations. The Secretary-General shall thereupon communicate the proposed amendment to States Parties, with a request that they indicate whether they favour a conference of States Parties for the purpose of considering and voting upon the proposals. In the event that, within four months from the date of such communication, at least one third of the States Parties favour such a conference, the Secretary-General shall convene the conference under the auspices of the United Nations. Any amendment adopted by a majority of States Parties present and voting at the

notification a été reçue par le Secrétaire général.

2. La dénonciation ne dégage pas l'État Partie qui en est l'auteur des obligations que lui impose le Protocole au regard de toute infraction survenue avant la date à laquelle la dénonciation prend effet, pas plus qu'elle n'entrave en aucune manière la poursuite de l'examen de toute question dont le Comité des droits de l'enfant serait déjà saisi avant cette date.

Article 16

1. Tout État Partie peut proposer un amendement et en déposer le texte auprès du Secrétaire général de l'Organisation des Nations Unies. Celui-ci communique alors la proposition d'amendement aux États Parties, en leur demandant de lui faire savoir s'ils sont favorables à la convocation d'une conférence des États Parties en vue de l'examen de la proposition et de sa mise aux voix. Si, dans les quatre mois qui suivent la date de cette communication, un tiers au moins des États Parties se prononcent en faveur de la convocation d'une telle conférence, le Secrétaire général convoque la conférence sous les auspices

conference shall be submitted to the General Assembly for approval.

2. An amendment adopted in accordance with paragraph I of the present Article shall enter into force when it has been approved by the General Assembly of the United Nations and accepted by a two-thirds majority of States Parties.

3. When an amendment enters into force, it shall be binding on those States Parties that have accepted it, other States Parties still being bound by the provisions of the present Protocol and any earlier amendments that they have accepted.

Article 17

1. The present Protocol, of which the Arabic, Chinese, English, French, Russian and Spanish texts are equally authentic, shall be deposited in the archives of the United Nations.

2. The Secretary-General of the United Nations shall transmit certified copies of the present Protocol to all States Parties to the Convention and all States that have signed the Convention.

de l'Organisation des Nations Unies. Tout amendement adopté par la majorité des États Parties présents et votants à la conférence est soumis à l'Assemblée générale des Nations Unies pour approbation.

2. Tout amendement adopté conformément aux dispositions du paragraphe 1 du présent article entre en vigueur lorsqu'il a été approuvé par l'Assemblée générale et accepté par une majorité des deux tiers des États Parties.

3. Lorsqu'un amendement entre en vigueur, il a force obligatoire pour les États Parties qui l'ont accepté, les autres États Parties demeurant liés par les dispositions du présent Protocole et par tous amendements antérieurs acceptés par eux.

Article 17

1. Le présent Protocole, dont les textes anglais, arabe, chinois, espagnol, français et russe font également foi, sera déposé aux archives de l'Organisation des Nations Unies.

2. Le Secrétaire général de l'Organisation des Nations Unies transmettra une copie certifiée conforme du présent Protocole à tous les États Parties à la Convention et à tous les États qui l'ont signée.

CHAPTER ONE

INTRODUCTION

1.1 *Background*

With the adoption of the UN Convention on the Rights of the Child on 20 November 1989 (hereafter CRC),[1] the first international human rights treaty of its time conceptualised the full scale of prevention and response mechanisms for different forms of violence, abuse and exploitation of children. At the same time, the UN Commission was deeply concerned about the existence of grave child rights violations in the form of commercial sexual exploitation of children worldwide.[2] It responded by appointing the first Special Rapporteur on the sale of children, child prostitution and child pornography[3] (hereafter: Special Rapporteur) in 1990, whose task it was to submit a report on the frequency and extent of such practices, as well as conclusions and recommendations.[4] As a response to this report, the Commission established a working group in 1994, with the mandate to develop guidelines for a potential draft optional protocol to the CRC focusing on combatting commercial sexual exploitation of children.[5]

Considering that sale of children and child sexual exploitation were already covered broadly in the CRC (Arts 19, 34–36 CRC), the possibility of a draft protocol on these issues was not supported by everyone, and interestingly, in particular not by the CRC Committee, the body of experts mandated to monitor the implementation of the CRC.[6] The CRC Committee, amongst others, was concerned that the Protocol might contradict or dilute the efforts of the CRC: a concern which, as we will discuss later in more detail, was not entirely far-fetched. Six working group

---

[1] Adopted and opened for signature, ratification and accession by General Assembly resolution 44/25 of 20 November 1989.

[2] Commission on Human Rights, *Sale of Children*, E/CN.4/RES/1990/68 (7 March 1990), p. 1.

[3] Now called 'Special Rapporteur on the sale and sexual exploitation of children', see https://www.ohchr.org/en/issues/children/pages/childrenindex.aspx (last accessed: 4 January 2022).

[4] Commission on Human Rights, *Sale of Children*, E/CN.4/RES/1990/68 (7 March 1990), p. 2.

[5] Wouter Vandenhole/Gamze Erdem Türkelli/Sara Lembrechts, *Children's Rights. A Commentary on the Rights of the Child and its Optional Protocol*, Cheltenham 2019, p. 447; John Tobin, *The Optional Protocol on the Sale of Children, Child Prostitution, and Child Pornography* in: John Tobin (ed.), *The UN Convention on the Rights of the Child: A Commentary*, Oxford 2019, p. 1713.

[6] Tobin, *The Optional Protocol on the Sale of Children, Child Prostitution, and Child Pornography*, p. 1714.

© KONINKLIJKE BRILL NV, LEIDEN, 2022 | DOI:10.1163/9789004460393_002

sessions and many hours of heated debate later, the working group had prepared
a draft Optional Protocol on the sale of children, child prostitution and child pornography (hereafter OPSC) which, despite partially fulfilling the concerns of the
CRC Committee raised above, provides for a comprehensive catalogue of state
obligations with a greatly needed focus on law enforcement collaboration and
child-centred justice which can be considered visionary for its time.[7] The OPSC
was eventually adopted by the United Nations General Assembly on 25 May 2000
and entered into force on 18 January 2002 in accordance with Art 14 OPSC.[8,9]

1.2 Impact of Globalisation and Digital Technologies

Even though globalisation and digital technologies were already starting to change
the national and international landscape in the 1990s and early 2000s when the
OPSC was drafted, the working group could not foresee the great impact globalisation, digital technologies and a world-wide pandemic would have on the sale
and sexual exploitation of children thirty years down the line. Since the OPSC
was adopted, the forms and scale of sale and sexual exploitation of children have
been constantly evolving.[10] Exchanging files on the Internet was just beginning
in the 1990s, and international travel was not as accessible and affordable as it is
today.[11] Whereas transnational elements of sale and sexual exploitation of children were the exception, they are now the rule. This has not only changed the
offending behaviour, but also demanded from the international community to
move away from national approaches and develop a truly transnational prevention and response network.[12]

As international travel became more available and accessible, the phenomenon
of travelling sex offenders emerged. These offenders often come from the Global

---

[7] Tobin, *The Optional Protocol on the Sale of Children, Child Prostitution, and Child Pornography*, p. 1714.
   [8] Please note that all articles in this commentary are those of the OPSC unless cited otherwise.
   [9] United Nations General Assembly, *Optional Protocols to the Convention on the Rights of the Child on the Involvement of Children in Armed Conflict and on the Sale of Children, Child Prostitution and Child Pornography* A/RES/54.263 (25 May 2000).
   [10] CRC Committee, *Guidelines regarding the implementation of the Optional Protocol to the Convention on the Rights of the Child on the sale of children, child prostitution and child pornography*, CRC/C/156 (10 September 2019), para. 2.
   [11] UNICEF Innocenti, *Handbook on the Optional Protocol on the Sale of Children, Child Prostitution and Child Pornography*, Florence 2009, p. viii.
   [12] Citing the risk of offenders targeting children in 'weaker' jurisdictions, WeProtect Global Alliance, *Global Threat Assessment 2021*, London 2021, p. 29.

North[13] to exploit children (and their families) from the Global South.[14] Travelling sex offenders increasingly use networks on the darknet[15] to target children in destination countries.[16] Globalisation has further led to the development of international adoption and international surrogacy as possible forms of sale of children, with a similar Global North–Global South dynamic. In addition, some orphanages are run as sale of children and/or child trafficking operations, capitalising the idea of 'white saviourism' for volunteers from—again—the Global North. However, not only the offenders are travelling, but also children. Increasingly driven into internal or cross-border migration by the impact of poverty and more recently of climate change and other extreme environmental events, children on the move are particularly vulnerable to sale and sexual exploitation if they are unaccompanied or separated from their families, and this vulnerability is further exacerbated by the limited access to services and justice.[17]

The widespread use and accessibility of the Internet has transformed the way child sexual abuse material is produced, shared and accessed. While this kind of material was initially produced and shared as hard copies, the Internet has revolutionised the market of child sexual abuse materials and now offers an unimaginable quantity and variety of harmful materials.[18] At the same time, it provides for easy ways to hide one's identity and sexually exploit children online, without creating any significant traces and hence minimising the risk to be prosecuted.[19]

---

[13] The term 'Global North' covers the G8 countries, the United States, Canada, all member states of the European Union, Israel, Japan, Singapore, South Korea, Australia, New Zealand and four of the five permanent members of the United Nations Security Council, excluding China, as defined in WeProtect Global Alliance, *Global Threat Assessment 2021*, p. 71.

[14] The term 'Global South' includes Africa, Latin America, the Middle East and developing Asia. This includes three of the four newly advanced economies of the BRIC countries (excluding Russia), which are Brazil, India and China, as defined in WeProtect Global Alliance, *Global Threat Assessment 2021*, p. 71.

[15] The darknet or dark web is the portion of the internet which can only get accessed through overlay networks such as VPN or peer-to-peer file sharing networks, see WeProtect Global Alliance, *Global Threat Assessment 2021*, p. 71.

[16] CRC Committee, *Guidelines regarding the implementation of the Optional Protocol to the Convention on the Rights of the Child on the sale of children, child prostitution and child pornography*, CRC/C/156, para. 3.

[17] UNICEF Innocenti, *The sale and sexual exploitation of children: Migration*, Florence 2020, pp. 2–3; Maud de Boer-Buquiccio/Maria Grazia Giammarinaro, *Joint report of the Special Rapporteur on the sale and sexual exploitation of children, including child prostitution, child pornography and other child sexual abuse material and the Special Rapporteur on trafficking in persons, especially women and children*, A/72/164 (18 July 2017).

[18] As an example, more than 3,000,000 accounts are registered across the 10 most harmful child sexual abuse sites on the dark web according to WeProtect Global Alliance, *Global Threat Assessment 2021*, p. 4; Alisdair A. Gillespie, *Child Pornography. Law and Policy*, London 2011, p. 5.

[19] UNODC, *Study on the Effects of New Information Technologies on the Abuse of Children*, New York 2015, p. 19.

While in the 1990s the working group discussed whether the 'mere' possession of child sexual abuse material should be criminalised under the OPSC,[20] we are now living in a time where people are sexually abusing and exploiting children via live stream, directing the form of abuse they want to see displayed from the comfort of their homes, and paying the facilitator of this live webcam child sexual exploitation through unregistered credit cards or digital currencies.[21] At the same time, digital technologies are shaping the experience of children across all aspects of their lives, with many of them growing up in a digitalised world from the day they were born (and even while still *in utero*).[22] This impacts the way children interact, relate and socialise with other people, and also the way they explore their sexuality both online and offline.[23] This poses difficult questions for the OPSC and the international community about balancing children's right to privacy with their right to protection from all forms of violence, abuse and exploitation, in particular in relation to the online sphere.

1.3 *Impact of COVID-19*

In addition to the all-encompassing globalisation and digitalisation of our lives, the global COVID-19 pandemic which hit the world in late 2019/early 2020 is considered one of the greatest shocks to global stability since World War II.[24] While children's health is generally considered to be less affected if they contract COVID-19 according to the current status of research, they are severely impacted by the measures Governments around the world have put in place to contain its spread.[25] Across the globe, countries effected lockdown measures, leading to highly restricted movement for a considerable period of time. Public offices shut down and public transport was disrupted, leading to considerable barriers to access services. Community support and child-care services were shut or were operating remotely.[26] At the same time, in cases of intra-family abuse, children

[20] UN Economic and Social Council, *Question of a draft optional protocol to the Convention on the Rights of the Child on the sale of children, child prostitution and child pornography, as well as the basic measures needed for their eradication*, E/CN.4/1998/103 (24 March 1998), para. 49; Gillespie, *Child Pornography. Law and Policy*, p. 98.

[21] UNODC, *Study on the Effects of New Information Technologies on the Abuse of Children*, pp. 21 et seq.

[22] UNICEF, *The State of the World's Children 2017*, New York 2017, p. 8.

[23] David Smahel/Kaveri Subrahmanyam, *Adolescent Sexuality on the Internet: A Developmental Perspective* in: Fabian M. Saleh/Albert J. Grudzinskas/Abigail M. Judge, *Adolescent sexual behavior in the digital era*, Oxford 2014, p. 65.

[24] Joining Forces, *Ending Violence against Children and COVID-19*, June 2019, p. 3.

[25] United Nations, *Policy Brief: The Impact of COVID-19 on children*, New York 2020, p. 4.

[26] Joining Forces, *Ending Violence against Children and COVID-19*, June 2019, p. 4.

were locked up with their perpetrators, leaving them in many situations without any protection or possibility of detection.[27] Lockdown measures, pausing of prevention programmes and increased economic hardship also have a dire effect on child marriages, which can amount to the sale of children.[28] Experts estimate that an additional 13 million child marriages could take place between 2020 and 2030 which otherwise would not have occurred.[29] Previous crises show that most of these marriages will take place in the first two years after the crisis took place, putting 4 million girls at immediate risk.[30] With the closure of schools and the shift to online learning, children spent more time online to learn and socialise, while not necessarily being educated on how to navigate online risks. This might expose them to increased levels of harm online.[31] Parents might either not be educated themselves on how to identify online risks for their children or be too occupied to provide the necessary support while juggling work, home schooling and care work. In addition, boredom and isolation might lead children to more risk-taking behaviour online.[32]

Offenders are similarly likely to increase the time spent online.[33] In the case of transnational sex offenders, the travel restrictions might lead them to shift their offending to the online environment.[34] Considering the economic impact COVID-19 has on the families across the globe, sale of children and their commercial sexual exploitation online might increase due to the precarious impact containment measures have on families' financial stability.[35] Shifting the perspective to law enforcement, investigators across the globe faced challenges to conduct investigations into these types of offences while working from home, and the reporting

---

[27] UNICEF, *Global COVID-19 Final Report*, New York 2021, pp. 3 et seq.

[28] CRC Committee, *Guidelines regarding the implementation of the Optional Protocol to the Convention on the Rights of the Child on the sale of children, child prostitution and child pornography*, CRC/C/156, para. 51.

[29] Mama Fatima Singhateh, *Report of the Special Rapporteur on the sale and sexual exploitation of children, including child prostitution, child pornography and other child sexual abuse material*, A/HRC/46/31 (22 January 2021), para. 38.

[30] Joining Forces, *Ending Violence against Children and COVID-19*, p. 5.

[31] CRC Committee, *General comment No. 25 (2021) on children's rights in relation to the digital environment*, CRC/C/GC/25 (2 March 2021), para. 80.

[32] INTERPOL, *Threats and Trends Child Sexual Abuse and Exploitation: COVID-19 Impact*, Lyon 2020, p. 6.

[33] India is reporting a 95% increase in searches for child sexual abuse material on the internet and Australia an 129% increase of reports of child sexual abuse material discovered, see WeProtect Global Alliance, *Global Threat Assessment 2021*, London 2021, p. 23.

[34] INTERPOL, *Threats and Trends Child Sexual Abuse and Exploitation: COVID-19 Impact*, Lyon 2020, p. 13; WeProtect Global Alliance, *Global Threat Assessment 2021*, p. 24.

[35] Singhateh, *Report of the Special Rapporteur on the sale and sexual exploitation of children, including child prostitution, child pornography and other child sexual abuse material*, A/HRC/46/31, paras. 15 et seq.; INTERPOL, *Threats and Trends Child Sexual Abuse and Exploitation: COVID-19 Impact*, p. 13.

behaviour of internet service providers was also negatively impacted due to the working-from-home modality.[36] With regards to online child sexual abuse and exploitation, INTERPOL identified some alarming trends which will significantly shape the next years of prevention and response: an increase in online child sexual exploitation and abuse activities on the darknet and clear web,[37] increased sharing of files through peer-to-peer services, and an increase in the distribution of self-generated material.[38] While the long-term consequences of COVID-19 on children's lives are not yet fully visible, the Special Rapporteur warned that 'children may well be among the biggest victims of the crisis [...], because their education, safety and health will be significantly undermined by the socioeconomic impact and by unintended consequences of the pandemic response'.[39]

1.4   Cross-Cutting Themes

Before diving into the in-depth analysis of the OPSC, it is important to conceptualise the interpretation of the OPSC in three cross-cutting themes: reminding the reader of the online-offline nexus, the need for a holistic gender lens, and particular attention towards Global North–Global South[40] dynamics.

1.4.1   Online-Offline Nexus

When access to and usage of the Internet started steeply increasing, and reports about online child sexual abuse and exploitation started hitting the news channels, a sheer panic about children's online activities emerged, resulting often times in overly restrictive policies that undermine children's online opportunities.[41] This protection-driven narrative failed to pay attention to the fact that *all* children's

---

[36] INTERPOL, *Threats and Trends Child Sexual Abuse and Exploitation: COVID-19 Impact*, p. 6.

[37] 'Clear web' or 'surface web' refers to the portion of the web which is accessible to the general public, see WeProtect Global Alliance, *Global Threat Assessment 2021*, p. 71.

[38] INTERPOL, *Threats and Trends Child Sexual Abuse and Exploitation: COVID-19 Impact*, p. 15 et seq.; for an interesting research project on child sexual abuse material consumers on the dark web, see Suojellaan Lapsia, *CSAM Users in the Dark Web. Protecting Children through Prevention*, Helsinki 2021.

[39] Singhateh, *Impact of coronavirus disease on different manifestations of sale and sexual exploitation of children. Report of the special rapporteur on the sale and exploitation of children, including child prostitution, child pornography and other child sexual abuse material*, A/HRC/46/3, para. 13; further noting that the reduction in global aid towards Global South countries as a consequence of the economic crises in many donor countries might further exacerbate the negative impact of COVID-19 on children's rights, WeProtect Global Alliance, *Global Threat Assessment 2021*, p. 25.

[40] For definitions of the 'Global North'–'Global South' terminology in this context, see WeProtect Global Alliance, *Global Threat Assessment 2019*, p. 4.

[41] Sonia Livingstone/Monica E. Bulger, *A Global Agenda for Children's Rights in the Digital Era. Recommendations for Developing UNICEF's Research Strategy*, Florence 2013, p. 4.

rights contained in the CRC are heavily influenced by the digital environment and globalisation, in particular children's rights to privacy, expression, access to information, and education, and hence need to be equally realised online. The promulgation of two separate, distinct 'online' and 'offline' 'worlds' are an artificial construct which does not reflect children's lived realities.[42] This recognition is important when discussing prevention and response to sale and sexual exploitation of children, as these offences tend to combine both online and offline components and hence require a holistic conceptualisation beyond online-offline binaries.[43] Considering the importance of General Comment No. 25 in conceptualising children's rights in the digital environment, it is unfortunate that it does not take a specific stance on this subject matter. Many countries still perceive children's rights in the digital environment to be a complete new set of rights compared to children's rights 'as we know them'. An explicit conceptualisation of the online-offline nexus would have been helpful to foster a holistic understanding of children's rights in today's digitalised and globalised world.

1.4.2 *Holistic Gender Lens*

Further, it is important to recognise that the sale and sexual exploitation of children were long understood to be 'girls' issues. Considering the persistent vulnerability of girls and their disproportionate representation in victim statistics in the context of these offences,[44] a focus on this group of children is necessary yet should not be misunderstood to be interchangeable with a gender perspective. Boys' vulnerability is often times masked as a strength and hence not considered as such: being socialised in patriarchal societies where 'boys don't cry' and grappling with harmful expectations posed onto them under the guise of 'masculinity', boys often times suffer in silence when experiencing violence.[45] As the Special Rapporteur

---

[42] Sabine K. Witting, *Walking a tightrope on an ethernet cable. The CRC Committee's 25th General Comment Children's Rights in relation to the digital environment*, Leiden Law Blog, 2nd April 2021, available here: https://leidenlawblog.nl/articles/walking-a-tightrope-on-an-ethernet-cable (last accessed: 15 October 2021).

[43] Daniel Kardefelt-Winther/Catherine Maternowska, *Addressing violence against children online and offline*, Nature Human Behaviour (2019).

[44] In 2019 and 2020, 92% and 93% of children depicted in child sexual abuse material analysed by the Internet Watch Foundation respectively were females, see Internet Watch Foundation, *The Annual Report 2020*, available here: https://www.iwf.org.uk/report/iwf-2020-annual-report-face-facts; CRC Committee, *Guidelines regarding the implementation of the Optional Protocol to the Convention on the Rights of the Child on the sale of children, child prostitution and child pornography*, CRC/C/156, para. 4.

[45] Christine Ricardo/Gary Bake, *Men, Masculinities, Sexual Exploitation and Sexual Violence. A Literature Review and Call for Action*, Washington 2008, pp. 16–17; UNICEF, *Research on the Sexual Exploitation of Boys: Findings, ethical considerations and methodological challenges*, New York 2020, pp. 6 et seq.

points out in her 2020 report, '[t]here are complex, ingrained and interrelated gaps linked to deep personal identity issues for boys around their masculinity and sexuality that prevent disclosure.'[46] This paired with an 'unwitting professional blindness on the part of some workers to indicators of exploitation in boys owing to the gendered expectations about the context of sexual exploitation,'[47] means there is urgent need to rethink the true gender-responsiveness of strategies employed to combat the sale and sexual exploitation of children.

This further requires paying special attention to children 'who identify outside the gender binary,'[48] as well as 'lesbian, gay, bisexual, transgender and intersex children'[49] and their experiences in the context of sale and sexual exploitation of children.[50] The specific recognition of sexuality diverse and gender diverse children resonates with evidence that suggests LGBTIQ+[51] children are both more likely to be sexually violated online and are more severely impacted by it. LGBTIQ+ children are more likely to look for sexual health information and explore their sexuality online.[52] Online sexual exploration might feel safer for this group of children and in many parts of the world, be the only space where they can explore their sexuality altogether, with the least fear of persecution. This search for positive sexual identity online puts LGBTIQ+ children at higher risk of being taken advantage of.[53] At the same time, evidence suggests that LGBTIQ+

---

[46] Mama Fatima Singhateh, *Report of the Special Rapporteur on the sale and sexual exploitation of children, including child prostitution, child pornography and other child sexual abuse material*, A/75/210 (21 July 2021), para. 19.

[47] Ibid., para. 19.

[48] Ibid., para. 39.

[49] CRC Committee, *General comment No. 25 (2021) on children's rights in relation to the digital environment*, CRC/C/GC/25, para 11; CRC Committee, *Guidelines regarding the implementation of the Optional Protocol to the Convention on the Rights of the Child on the sale of children, child prostitution and child pornography*, CRC/C/156, para. 13.

[50] Identifying LGBTQ++ children as specifically vulnerable in the context of online child sexual abuse and exploitation, WeProtect Global Alliance, *Global Threat Assessment 2019*, p. 29.

[51] The term 'LGBTIQ' stands for 'Lesbian, Gay, Bisexual, Transsexual, Intersexual, Queer'. The '+' is added to cover any other sexual orientations or gender identities which do not fall under the above identifications.

[52] Corinne May-Chahal/Emma Palmer, *Rapid Evidence Assessment. Characteristics and vulnerabilities of victims of online-facilitated child sexual abuse and exploitation*, Lancaster 2018, p. 48; Tink Palmer, *Digital dangers. The impact of technology on the sexual abuse and exploitation of children and young people*, Ilford 2015, p. 33.

[53] Mitchell Kimberly/Michelle Ybarra/Josephine Korchmaros, *Sexual harassment among adolescents of different sexual orientation and gender identities*, Child Abuse and Neglect, Vol. 38 (2014), p. 285; May-Chahal/ Palmer, *Rapid Evidence Assessment. Characteristics and vulnerabilities of victims of online-facilitated child sexual abuse and exploitation*, p. 48; according to a study, Flemish teens who identify as LGBTIQ+ were more often pressured into sharing sexually explicit material of themselves compared to their heterosexual peers, see WeProtect Global Alliance, *Global Threat Assessment 2021*, p. 56.

children suffer from more severe impact of the online violence, as it adds to the already existing stress of belonging to a sexual minority and an increased feeling of being unsafe.[54]

1.4.3 Global North–Global South Dynamic

Lastly, it is important to note the large majority of research which has been conducted on the topics of sale and sexual exploitation of children, in particular in the context of online offending, originates from the Global North.[55] This influences the discourse in various ways: it neglects the voices, experiences and individualities of children from the Global South and assumes that strategies which have worked in the Global North are equally effective and relevant for Global South contexts.[56] This is particularly concerning as the victims of transnational sexual offences in many cases are children from the Global South, abused by perpetrators from the Global North.[57] Further, this dynamic plays an important role in the context of 'voluntourism' or 'orphanage tourism', which predominantly affects the Global South and which might result in the sale and sexual exploitation of children in these countries.[58] In the context of online child sexual abuse and exploitation, the majority of children identified in abuse imagery are from North America and Western Europe, however, when shifting the focus to emerging forms such as livestreaming, the majority of the victims is from the Global South.[59] Therefore, special attention needs to be paid to these Global North-Global South dynamics, to ensure the voices of children from the Global South are equally weighed in the discourse.

---

[54] Kimberly/Ybarra/Korchmaros, *Sexual harassment among adolescents of different sexual orientation and gender identities*, p. 291.

[55] Recent research studies on online child sexual abuse and exploitation in the Global South are an important step to change this predominant research focus, see ECPAT/INTERPOL/UNICEF, *Disrupting harm in Kenya: Evidence on online child sexual exploitation and abuse*, Bangkok/Lyon/Florence 2021; ECPAT/INTERPOL/UNICEF, *Disrupting harm in Uganda: Evidence on online child sexual exploitation and abuse*, Bangkok/Lyon/Florence 2021; ECPAT/INTERPOL/UNICEF, *Disrupting harm in Thailand: Evidence on online child sexual exploitation and abuse*, Bangkok/Lyon/Florence 2022; ECPAT/INTERPOL/UNICEF, *Disrupting harm in Tanzania: Evidence on online child sexual exploitation and abuse*, Bangkok/Lyon/Florence 2022; ECPAT/INTERPOL/UNICEF, *Disrupting harm in Ethiopia: Evidence on online child sexual exploitation and abuse*, Bangkok/Lyon/Florence 2022; ECPAT/INTERPOL/UNICEF, *Disrupting harm in the Philippines: Evidence on online child sexual exploitation and abuse*, Bangkok/Lyon/Florence 2022.

[56] Livingstone/ Bulger, *A Global Agenda for Children's Rights in the Digital Era. Recommendations for Developing UNICEF's Research Strategy*, p. 21.

[57] ECPAT, *Global Study Report on Sexual Exploitation of Children in Travel and Tourism*, Bangkok 2016, pp. 56 et seq.

[58] ECPAT, *Explanatory Report to the Guidelines Regarding the Implementation of the Optional Protocol to the Convention on the Rights of the Child on the Sale of Children, Child Prostitution and Child Pornography*, Bangkok 2019, p. 49.

[59] WeProtect Global Alliance, *Global Threat Assessment 2021*, pp. 41, 60.

Applying the above cross-cutting themes as thematic lenses, this commentary will analyse and interpret the wording of each provision of the OPSC; provide for an interpretation most relevant in the context of today's globalised and digitalised world, leaning strongly on the CRC Committee *Guidelines regarding the implementation of the Optional Protocol to the Convention on the Rights of the Child on the sale of children, child prostitution and child pornography* (hereafter: the Guidelines)[60] and *General comment No. 25 (2021) on children's rights in relation to the digital environment*;[61] and showcase best practices for the standards laid out in the OPSC, to provide concrete examples for how the OPSC should be applied in States parties.

---

[60] CRC Committee, *Guidelines regarding the implementation of the Optional Protocol to the Convention on the Rights of the Child on the sale of children, child prostitution and child pornography*, CRC/C/156, adopted on 30 May 2019.

[61] CRC Committee, *General comment No. 25 (2021) on children's rights in relation to the digital environment*, CRC/C/GC/25, adopted on 24 March 2021.

CHAPTER TWO

COMPARISON WITH RELATED INTERNATIONAL HUMAN RIGHTS STANDARDS

2.1 *UN Convention on the Rights of the Child, 1989*

2.1.1 *Art 16 CRC: Right to Protection of Privacy, Family, Home, Correspondence, Honour and Reputation*

Art 16 CRC states the child's right to be protected from arbitrary or unlawful interference with their[62] privacy, family, home and correspondence. In the Guidelines, the CRC Committee highlights the importance of Art 16 CRC in the context of the OPSC by including it in its general measures of implementation, on the same level as the four core principles:

> The Committee emphasizes that any measure to implement the provisions on the Optional Protocol should fully comply with the Convention, in particular with the general principles contained in articles 2, 3, 6 and 12, as well as respecting the child's right to privacy.[63]

The first dimension of the influence of Art 16 CRC on the OPSC is the child's right to be protected from unlawful and arbitrary data processing. Data may hereby include 'children's identities, activities, location, communication, emotions, health and relationships'.[64] Possible violations of children's privacy and data occur in the context of online investigation of sale and sexual exploitation of children offences. A prominent example of a possible interference with children's right to privacy and data protection is the call for abolishment of end-to-end encryption for online messaging services, in order to continuously enable service providers and law enforcement to detect and investigate the sharing of child sexual abuse material on such networks.[65] While the investigation of such offences is obviously

---

[62] The gender-neutral pronoun 'they' (singular) is used throughout this publication to avoid the exclusion of non-binary children. Reference to 'boys' and 'girls' is made where this is relevant for the context or mandated by the cited source.

[63] CRC Committee, *Guidelines regarding the implementation of the Optional Protocol to the Convention on the Rights of the Child on the sale of children, child prostitution and child pornography*, CRC/C/156, para. 11.

[64] CRC Committee, *General comment No. 25 (2021) on children's rights in relation to the digital environment*, CRC/C/GC/25, para. 68.

[65] WeProtect Global Alliance, *Global Threat Assessment 2021*, p. 34; see also EU, *Proposal for a regulation of the European parliament and of the council laying down rules to prevent and combat*

© KONINKLIJKE BRILL NV, LEIDEN, 2022 | DOI:10.1163/9789004460393_003

a key strategy under the OPSC, it has to be considered that at the same time, end-to-end encryption benefits children's right to privacy and is hence a protected interest under Art 16 CRC. To solve this conflict, the CRC Committee in General Comment No. 25 states that 'where encryption is considered an appropriate means, States parties should consider appropriate measures enabling the detection and reporting of child sexual exploitation and abuse or child sexual abuse material. Such measures must be strictly limited according to the principles of legality, necessity and proportionality'.[66] Even though it is clear that the devil lies in the detail,[67] it is important to note that the CRC Committee is calling for a proportionate solution to this question, which to the best extent possible both protects the child's right to privacy and the child's right to be protected from all forms of violence, abuse and exploitation.[68]

The second aspect is the child's right to privacy in the context of age-appropriate, consensual sexual exploration. The wording of Art 16 CRC is modelled after Art 17 of the International Covenant on Civil and Political Rights, and according to the UN Human Rights Committee 'it is undisputed that adult consensual sexual activity in private is covered by the concept of privacy'.[69] The CRC Committee in its General Comment No. 4 on Adolescent Health and Development recognises that 'adolescence is a period characterised by rapid physical, cognitive and social changes, including sexual and reproductive maturation', acknowledging that challenges encountered by adolescents 'include developing an individual identity dealing with one's sexuality'.[70] When discussing States parties' obligation to set a minimum age of sexual consent, the CRC Committee stresses that 'these minimum ages [...] closely reflect the recognition of the status of human beings under 18 years of age as rights holders, in accordance with their evolving capacity, age and maturity (arts. 5 and 12 and 17)'.[71] Even though this statement does not clearly indicate whether consensual sexual relationships amongst children are protected under the right to privacy with the caveat of Arts 5, 12 and 17, it certainly indicates

---

child sexual abuse, 2022/0155(COD) (11 May 2022), which might lead to the *de facto* abolishment of end-to-end encryption on platforms.

[66] CRC Committee, *General comment No. 25 (2021) on children's rights in relation to the digital environment*, CRC/C/GC/25, para. 70.

[67] For a more detailed analysis of this subject matter see Daniel Kardefelt-Winther/Emma Day/Gabrielle Berman/Sabine K. Witting/Anjan Bose, *Encryption, Privacy and Children's Right to Protection from Harm*, Office of Research—Innocenti Working Paper, Florence 2020.

[68] For an overview of current technological developments in this field, see WeProtect Global Alliance, *Global Threat Assessment 2021*, p. 34.

[69] UN Human Rights Committee, *Tonnen v. Australia*, Communication No. 488/1992, U.N. Doc CCPR/C/50/D/488/1992 (1994), para. 8.2.

[70] CRC Committee, *General Comment No. 4: Adolescent Health and Development in the Context of the Convention on the Rights of the Child*, CRC/GC/2003/04 (1 July 2003), p. 1.

[71] Ibid., para. 5.

that children's evolving capacity and level of maturity plays a role regarding the extent to which legislative restrictions on consensual sexual activity of children can be imposed.[72] In the context of the OPSC, this is particularly relevant for the legal response to child 'self-generated' sexual material and the question whether the age of consent for offline sexual activity should align with the age of consent for online sexual activity (see section 3.2.2.4).

This clearly shows that the right to privacy affects the OPSC on various levels and should not be considered as a secondary right to children's right to protection from violence, abuse and exploitation.[73] A careful balancing between Art 16 CRC and the child's rights under Art 19, 34–36 CRC is therefore crucial to do justice to the principle of evolving capacities set out in Art 5 CRC.[74]

2.1.2 Art 19 CRC: The Right to Protection against All Forms of Violence

Art 19 CRC stipulates that 'States Parties shall take all appropriate legislative, administrative, social and educational measures to protect the child from all forms of physical or mental violence, injury or abuse, neglect or negligent treatment, maltreatment or exploitation, including sexual abuse, while in the care of parent(s), legal guardian(s) or any other person who has the care of the child'. From a conceptual point of view, the CRC Committee takes a child-rights based approach to the protection of children against all forms of violence, highlighting the importance of seeing children as active right-holders rather than perceiving them as 'victims' without any agency.[75] By moving away from such a 'welfare' approach, Art 19 CRC embodies a key paradigm shift in the protection of children.[76]

Regarding the terminology, 'violence' is understood as an umbrella term for all forms of harm listed in Art 19 (1) CRC, including non-intentional and non-physical forms of harm.[77] Importantly, Art 19 CRC focuses on violence occurring in intra-family and intra-institutional set ups, recognising that violence is often inflicted

---

[72] John Tobin/Sarah M. Field, *Art. 16. The Right to Protection of Privacy, Family, Home, Correspondence, Honour and Reputation* in John Tobin (ed.), *The UN Convention on the Rights of the Child: A Commentary*, Oxford 2019, p. 565.

[73] Witting, *Walking a tightrope on an ethernet cable. The CRC Committee's 25th General Comment Children's Rights in relation to the digital environment*, Leiden Law Blog, 2nd April 2021.

[74] CRC Committee, *General Comment No. 13: The right of the child to freedom from all forms of violence*, CRC/C/GC/13 (18 April 2011), para. 82.

[75] Ibid., para. 3.

[76] John Tobin/Judy Cashmore, *Art. 19 The Right to Protection from All Forms of Violence in:* John Tobin (ed.), *The UN Convention on the Rights of the Child: A Commentary*, Oxford 2019, p. 723.

[77] CRC Committee, *General Comment No. 13: The right of the child to freedom from all forms of violence*, CRC/C/GC/13, para. 4.

on children by members of their close family and community circles. However, the term 'any other person who has the care of the child' should not be interpreted too narrowly, but includes persons concerned with the obligation to care for a child, rather than the actual physical care.[78] This covers for example professionals employed in 'schools, care centres, residential homes, police custody and justice institutions'.[79] Notably, Art 19 CRC puts a strong focus on both prevention and response mechanisms, with the CRC Committee noting that 'preventive measures offer the greatest return in the long term. However, commitment to prevention does not lessen States' obligations to respond effectively to violence when it occurs'.[80] This holistic approach to ending violence against children is the second paradigm shift effected in Art 19 CRC, following an ecological rather than a pathological model.[81]

In conclusion, Art 19 CRC must be understood as the 'core provision for discussions and strategies to address and eliminate all forms of violence in the context of the Convention more broadly'[82] which also applies to violence against children committed through the use of ICTs,[83] and is hence guiding the interpretation of the OPSC.

2.1.3 *Art 21 CRC: Adoption*

Art 20 (3) CRC names adoption as one of various forms of alternative care for children temporarily or permanently deprived of their family environment. Conscious of the prohibition of adoption under Islamic law, Art 21 CRC only mandates States Parties which recognize and/or permit adoption to ensure that the best interests of the child shall be the paramount consideration. Art 21 a) CRC states that the adoption needs to be authorised by the relevant authority, which is mandated to investigate whether the adoption is permissible in the view of the child's status and that if required, informed consent by the persons concerned has been given. Art 21 b)–d) CRC regulate inter-country adoption, stating that inter-country adoption should be a measure of last resort; that children concerned by inter-country adoption enjoy the same safeguards and standards as is the case for intra-country adoption; and that States parties should take all appropriate measures to ensure that the placement does not result in improper financial gain.

---

[78] Tobin/ Cashmore, *Art. 19 The Right to Protection from All Forms of* Violence, p. 691.

[79] CRC Committee, *General Comment No. 13: The right of the child to freedom from all forms of violence*, CRC/C/GC/13, para. 3.

[80] Ibid.

[81] Tobin/ Cashmore, *Art. 19 The Right to Protection from All Forms of Violence*, p. 723.

[82] CRC Committee, *General Comment No. 13: The right of the child to freedom from all forms of violence*, CRC/C/GC/13, para. 7.

[83] Ibid., para. 31.

Highlighting the devastating impact of child adoption operations for commercial purposes, certain forms of adoption can be considered sale of children as defined in Art 2 and hence fall under the scope of Art 3. This will be further discussed in section 3.2.2.2.

Art 21 CRC and the OPSC hence need to be closely read together, and the OPSC complements Art 21 CRC insofar as it requires States parties to criminalise illegal adoptions which are considered sale of children as set out in Art 2.

2.1.4 *Art 34 CRC: Protection from Sexual Exploitation and Sexual Abuse*

Art 34 CRC is the main provision on protection of children from sexual exploitation and abuse. It states:

> States Parties undertake to protect the child from all forms of sexual exploitation and sexual abuse. For these purposes, States Parties shall in particular take all appropriate national, bilateral and multilateral measures to prevent:
> a) The inducement or coercion of a child to engage in any unlawful sexual activity;
> b) The exploitative use of children in prostitution or other unlawful sexual practices;
> c) The exploitative use of children in pornographic performances and material.

Firstly, it is important to note that the CRC does not define the terms 'sexual abuse' or 'sexual exploitation'. However, the Committee recommends to states that 'clear operational legal definitions are required of the different forms of violence in all settings.'[84] Guidance on defining these terms can be drawn from the WHO Report on Child Abuse Prevention[85] and the so-called 'Luxembourg Guidelines'.[86]

Art 34 a) CRC requires States parties to prevent the inducement or coercion of a child to engage in any unlawful sexual activity. It is interesting to note that only inducement to engage in any *unlawful* activity is prohibited under the CRC. This indicates that the CRC does not consider every sexual activity with a child to be automatically unlawful. Having said that, the 'unlawfulness' criteria of Art 34 a) CRC is nonetheless redundant. If any form of inducement or coercion is present, sexual activity with a child (or with any other person for that matter) should

---

[84] CRC Committee, *General Comment No. 13: The right of the child to freedom from all forms of violence*, CRC/C/GC/13, para. 18.

[85] WHO, *Report of the Consultation on Child Abuse Prevention*, Geneva 1999.

[86] ECPAT, *Terminology Guidelines for the Protection of Children from Sexual Exploitation and Sexual Abuse*, Bangkok 2016; Common understanding is hereby that 'sexual abuse' of a child requires sexual activity with a child under some form of 'abusive condition', such as force, grooming, inducement, threats or a large age gap between the child and the sexual partner. 'Sexual exploitation' is understood to include sexual activity with a child which includes some form of (commercial) exchange, see John Tobin/Florence Seow, *Art. 34 Protection from Sexual Exploitation and Sexual Abuse* in: John Tobin (ed.), *The UN Convention on the Rights of the Child: A Commentary*, Oxford 2019, p. 1316 et seq.

never be considered lawful as the person did not give its free and informed consent but was 'induced' or 'coerced'.

Nonetheless, the spirit of considering sexual activity with a child to be lawful under certain circumstances is further repeated in Art 34 b) and c) CRC, which only prohibits the *exploitative* use of children in prostitution or pornography. This means that at least in theory, children could participate in prostitution or pornographic performances if they give free and informed consent and are not exploited in the process. While the CRC at least seems to consider that sexual exploration might extend to children's participation in prostitution and pornography if no exploitative element is present, the OPSC takes a very clear stance against a child's ability to consent to participating in prostitution or pornography. Art 2 prohibits any form of 'child prostitution' and 'child pornography', regardless of whether it is considered exploitative or not. This resembles a return to the welfare approach which the CRC intended to abolish in its Arts 19, 34–36 CRC.

This contradiction between the OPSC and the CRC is not only an academic problem but becomes increasingly relevant in cases of consensual online sexual activity between peers ('sexting') as well as children's online participation in commercial sex. The CRC Committee's stance on these subject matters will be discussed in-depth in sections 3.2.2.3 and 3.2.2.4.

Lastly, it is important to note that Art 34 CRC complements the OPSC by requiring States parties to take all appropriate measures to protect children from all forms of sexual exploitation and abuse. Read in conjunction with Art 4 CRC, this can be interpreted to include an obligation to put in place legal measures which go beyond the legal obligations set out in the OPSC. Beyond the OPSC legal requirements for criminalisation, jurisdiction, extradition, mutual legal assistance (MLA), prevention and international collaboration (Arts 2, 3, 4, 5, 6, 9 and 10), further legal measures are required to ensure that offenders are brought to book. As an example, this includes mandatory reporting, notice and take down procedures for Internet Service Providers which discover child sexual abuse materials on their platforms or criminal procedure rules for admissibility of digital evidence or undercover investigations on the darknet. While such legal measures are not explicitly covered under the OPSC, they can be considered a complementary requirement under Arts 34, 4 CRC.

2.1.5 *Art 35 CRC: Protection against Abduction, Traffic and Sale of Children*

Art 35 CRC states that 'States parties shall take all appropriate national, bilateral and multilateral measures to prevent the abduction, the sale of or traffic in

children for any purpose or in any form'. The CRC does not provide any definitions of the term 'abduction', which poses the question how it relates to Art 11 CRC. The CRC Committee seems to differentiate between 'illicit transfer and non-return of children abroad' under Art 11 CRC and 'abduction' under Art 35 CRC by conceptualising the latter in the context of an intended or actual exploitation of the child.[87] 'Sale of children' and 'trafficking in children' are also not defined in the CRC, however, a clear definition for 'sale of children' is put forward in the OPSC which will be discussed in-depth in section 3.2.2.2. While Art 35 CRC was the first of its kind to specifically cover 'child trafficking' and to consider other forms of exploitation outside sexual exploitation to form part of such offences, the 2000 Protocol to prevent, suppress, and punish trafficking in human beings, especially women and children (so-called Palermo Protocol), which supplements the UN Convention against Transnational Organized Crime, is now considered the main legal instrument to combat trafficking in persons.[88]

Despite the definitions in the OPSC and the Palermo Protocol, concepts of 'sale of children' and 'child trafficking' still cause confusion in practice as they are often wrongfully used interchangeably. This will be further discussed in section 3.2.2.2.

2.1.6 *Art 36 CRC: Protection against All Other Forms of Exploitation*

Art 36 CRC requires States Parties to 'protect the child against all other forms of exploitation prejudicial to any aspects of the child's wellbeing'. Art 36 CRC is considered a catch-all provision which becomes relevant if a specific form of exploitation is not covered under the *leges speciales* of Art 34, Art 35 CRC and the OPSC. Its function is therefore to avoid the creation of a legal vacuum by providing for an umbrella clause against all forms of child exploitation.[89]

2.2 *Council of Europe Cybercrime Convention ('Budapest Convention'), 2003*

The so-called Budapest Convention,[90] a treaty on cybercrime and international collaboration in this field, was initiated and drafted by members of the Council of Europe and is open for signature and ratification by its member states. However, it is also open for signature or ratification by non-Council of Europe member states that participated in its elaboration (Canada, Japan, South Africa and the

---

[87] Anne Gallagher, *Art. 35 Protection against the Abduction, Traffic, and Sale of Children* in: John Tobin (ed.), *The UN Convention on the Rights of the Child: A Commentary*, Oxford 2019, p. 1362.

[88] Gallagher, *Art. 35 Protection against the Abduction, Traffic, and Sale of Children*, p. 1357.

[89] John Tobin, *Art 36 Protection against All Other Forms of Exploitation* in John Tobin (ed.), *The UN Convention on the Rights of the Child: A Commentary*, Oxford 2019, p. 1403.

[90] Official title: Council of Europe Convention on Cybercrime.

US) and for accession by other non-member states. To date, the Convention has been ratified or acceded to by 67 States,[91] including key global cyberspace players such as the US and Canada and is therefore the most important international cybercrime convention. Amongst the various forms of cybercrimes regulated by the Convention is also a provision on 'child pornography'. Art 9(2) of the Budapest Convention defines 'child pornography' as 'pornographic material that visually depicts (a) a minor engaged in sexually explicit conduct; (b) a person appearing to be a minor engaged in sexually explicit conduct; (c) realistic images representing a minor engaged in sexually explicit conduct'.

Further, the Budapest Convention is the only international treaty with cyber-specific mutual legal assistance (MLA) and extradition provisions.[92] Chapter III (International cooperation) contains extradition provisions and a wide range of MLA ones that apply even where no MLA treaty exists between the parties. Specific provisional MLA regulations are complemented by a 24/7 network for speedy mutual assistance among parties. Further, Arts 29 and 30 the Budapest Convention set out provisional measures for the preservation of data, which take the volatile nature of digital evidence into account.[93] In addition, the Council of Europe recently adopted a Second Additional Protocol to the Convention on Cybercrime on enhanced co-operation and disclosure of electronic evidence, which provides a legal basis for disclosure of domain name registration information and for direct co-operation with service providers for subscriber information, effective means to obtain subscriber information and traffic data, immediate co-operation in emergencies, mutual assistance tools, as well as personal data protection safeguards.[94] The Optional Protocol has been open for signature and ratification since May 2022.[95]

The Budapest Convention sets therefore an important benchmark for transnational law enforcement collaboration, which will be more closely discussed in the context of Arts 5, 6 and 10.

---

[91] See status of ratifications/accessions here: https://www.coe.int/en/web/conventions/full-list/-/conventions/treaty/185/signatures (last accessed: 2 October 2022).

[92] Anna-Maria Osula, *Mutual Legal Assistance & Other Mechanisms for Accessing Extraterritorially Located Data*, Masaryk University Journal of Law and Technology, Vol. 9 (2015), p. 49.

[93] Osula, *Mutual Legal Assistance & Other Mechanisms for Accessing Extraterritorially Located Data*, p. 50.

[94] See full text here: https://search.coe.int/cm/pages/result_details.aspx?objectid=0900001680a48e4d (last accessed: 13 June 2022).

[95] 24 countries have so far signed the Additional Protocol, see https://www.coe.int/en/web/conventions/full-list?module=signatures-by-treaty&treatynum=224 (last accessed: 13 June 2022).

2.3   Council of Europe Convention on the Protection of Children against Sexual Exploitation and Sexual Abuse ('Lanzarote Convention'), 2007

The Lanzarote Convention[96] is an international treaty which aims to serve as 'comprehensive international instrument focusing on preventive, protective and criminal law aspects of the fight against all forms of sexual exploitation and sexual abuse of children and setting up a specific monitoring mechanism'.[97] It is open for signature and ratification by Council of Europe member states, and open for accession by non-Council of Europe member states. Currently, the Lanzarote Convention has 48 member states.[98]

Apart from prescribing a comprehensive set of preventive measures, the Convention makes provisions for the criminalisation of various sexual offences against children, such as 'Offences concerning child prostitution' (Art 19 Lanzarote Convention), 'Offences concerning child pornography' (Art 20 Lanzarote Convention), Offences concerning the participation of a child in pornographic performances' (Art 21 Lanzarote Convention) and 'Solicitation of children for sexual purposes' (Art 23 Lanzarote Convention). While an in-depth interpretation and analysis of the above provisions exceeds the scope of this commentary, it is important to note that the Lanzarote Convention was the first international treaty which clearly addressed the issue of consensual online sexual exploration of children ('sexting') in its Art 20 (3) Lanzarote Convention. This provision will be further discussed in the context of 'child pornography' under the OPSC in section 3.2.2.4.

Further, the Convention makes provision for the investigation and prosecution of above offences including procedural law, with a comprehensive provision on general measures of protection for child victims in Art 31 Lanzarote Convention. This provision is complemented by Art 35 Lanzarote Convention on interviewing child witnesses and Art 36 Lanzarote Convention on child-friendly criminal court proceedings. These procedural provisions will be discussed in more detail in the context of Art 8.

---

[96] Official title: Council of Europe Convention on Protection of Children against Sexual Exploitation and Sexual Abuse.

[97] Preamble, Lanzarote Convention.

[98] See status of ratifications/accessions here: https://www.coe.int/en/web/conventions/full-list2?module=signatures-by-treaty&treatynum=201 (last accessed: 9 September 2021).

2.4 *African Charter on the Rights and Welfare of the Child, 1990*

The African Charter on the Rights and Welfare of the Child (hereafter ACRWC) was adopted on 11 July 1990. The ACRWC currently has 50 member states.[99]

The reasoning for the adoption of an African children's rights instrument in addition to many African states ratifying the CRC, was that African states were grossly underrepresented in the drafting process of the CRC and hence felt that particularly 'African' issues were insufficiently reflected. Therefore, despite adopting the core content of many provisions of the CRC, additional focus was paid to the situation of children living under apartheid, the situation of the African girl child, harmful practices such as child marriages and female genital mutilation, the role of the community and the extended family as well as the use of child soldiers.[100]

Distinct African features are also prevalent in the provisions regulating the sexual exploitation and sale of children, namely Art 27 and Art 29 ACRWC. Art 27 ACRWC is modelled after Art 34 CRC, with a distinct difference: the terms 'exploitative' and 'unlawful' have been left out, hence eliminating the notion of the possibility of children's consent to participating in sexual activities, 'prostitution' or pornography. On paper, the ACRWC hence follows a similar protectionist view as the OPSC. However, it has to be noted that the African Committee of Experts on the Rights and Welfare of the Child (ACERWC) in its recently published General Comment No. 7 on Art 27 ACRWC takes a much more differentiated view, by acknowledging that consensual sexual activity amongst adolescents is not inherently harmful or exploitative and that the criminalisation of all sexual activity with a person below the age of 18 years, including adolescents, will not stop adolescents from engaging in sex, but rather drive the sexual activity underground and prevent adolescents from accessing sexual reproductive health services.[101] The General Comment makes the same exemption for consensual online sexual activity between adolescents, hence following international best practice as described in the Lanzarote Convention or in the OPSC Guidelines.[102] Against this background, General Comment No. 7 fundamentally changes the conceptualisation and interpretation of sexual abuse in the context of the ACRWC.

---

99 See status of ratifications here: https://www.acerwc.africa/ratifications-table/ (last accessed: 9 September 2021).

100 Julia Sloth-Nielsen, *The African Charter in the Rights and Welfare of the* Child in Trynie Boezaart (eds.), *Child Law in South Africa*, Johannesburg 2017, pp. 424–425; Thoko Kaime, *The Foundation of Rights in the African Charter on the Rights and Welfare of the Child: A Historical and Philosophical Account*, African Journal of Legal Studies, Vol. 3 (2009), pp. 131–132.

101 ACERWC, *General Comment No. 7 on Art 27 of the African Charter on the Rights and Welfare of the Child*, Maseru 2021, paras. 50 et seq.

102 Ibid., paras. 83 et seq.

Art 29 ACRWC requires member states to take all appropriate measures to prevent the abduction, sale of, or traffic in children for any purpose or in any form, by any person including parents or legal guardians of the child, and the use of children in all forms of begging. While the wording of the provision is very similar to Art 35 CRC, neither the CRC nor the OPSC make specific reference to the person who sells, abducts or traffics the child nor the use of children in all forms of begging. The ACRWC is therefore the first international human rights instrument which makes specific (yet limited) reference to children in street situations and their specific vulnerabilities to various forms of exploitation.[103]

2.5 *African Convention on Personal Data Protection and Cyber Security, 2015*

The AU adopted its Convention on Cyber Security and Personal Data Protection on 27 June 2014. Fifteen AU member states must ratify the Convention before it enters into force.[104] Currently, the Convention has been ratified by eight and signed by fourteen member states and is hence not operational yet.[105]

Art 1 of the Convention defines 'child pornography' as 'any visual depiction, including any photograph, film, video, image, whether made or produced by electronic, mechanical, or other means, of sexually explicit conduct, where a) the production of such visual depiction involves a minor; b) such visual depiction is a digital image, computer image, or computer-generated image where a minor is engaging in sexually explicit conduct or when images of their sexual organs are produced or used for primarily sexual purposes and exploited with or without the child's knowledge; c) such visual depiction has been created, adapted, or modified to appear that a minor is engaging in sexually explicit conduct'. It criminalises the producing, registering, manufacturing, disseminating, procuring and possessing of 'child pornography' and exposing minors to 'images, documents, sound or representation of a pornographic nature'.[106] Lastly, it requires states to strengthen

---

[103] Danwood Mzikenge Chirwa, *The merits and demerits of the African Charter on the Rights and Welfare of the Child*, International Journal of Children's Rights, Vol. 10 (2002), p. 166.

[104] Article 36 of the African Union Convention on Cyberspace Security and African Union Protection of Personal Data.

[105] See African Union 'List of countries which have signed, ratified/acceded to the African Union Convention on Cyber Security and Personal Data Protection' 20/06/2020, available at: https://au.int/sites/default/files/treaties/29560-sl-AFRICAN%20UNION%20CONVENTION%20ON%20CYBER%20SECURITY%20AND%20PERSONAL%20DATA%20PROTECTION.pdf (last accessed: 10 September 2021).

[106] African Convention on Cybersecurity and Personal Data Protection, Art. 29 3).

regional harmonisation and encourages the signing of mutual legal assistance agreements.[107]

2.6   *Hague Conventions (1980, 1993, 1996)*

In its preamble, the OPSC makes explicit reference to three Hague Conventions, namely the 1993 Hague Convention on the Protection of Children and Cooperation with Respect to Inter-Country Adoption, the 1980 Hague Convention on the Civil Aspects of International Child Abduction, and the 1996 Hague Convention on Jurisdiction, Applicable Law, Recognition, Enforcement and Cooperation in Respect of Parental Responsibility and Measures for the Protection of Children. Simultaneously, the Hague Convention on Intercountry Adoption and the Hague Convention on Jurisdiction consider the principles set forth in the Convention of the Rights of the Child.

This shows that the CRC and the Hague Conventions pursue the same objectives, namely, to ensure the protection of children in all intercountry matters by setting the best interests of the child as primary consideration. While the CRC in Art 21 and Art 11 calls upon States parties to conclude bi- and multi-lateral agreements to achieve the objectives set forth in these articles, the Hague Conventions can be seen as the practical instrument to realise this call by establishing a system of co-operation with minimum standards and safeguards.

Considering that the Hague Conventions were adopted before the OPSC was drafted and hence do not provide for a specific reference to the OPSC, the Hague Convention on Intercountry Adoption sets as one of its objectives to 'prevent the abduction, the sale of, or traffic in children' and hence clearly pursues the same objectives as the OPSC. The Hague Conventions and the OPSC's relation-ship is hereby complementary, with the Hague Conventions setting the civil law framework to regulate intercountry matters affecting children and the OPSC set-ting minimum standards for the criminalisation of intercountry practices which harm children. This linkage becomes explicit in Art 3 1) (a) (ii), which criminalises 'improperly inducing consent, as an intermediary, for the adoption of a child in violation of applicable international legal instruments on adoption'. One of the main international legal instruments on adoption is hereby the Hague Convention on Intercountry Adoption.

Worth mentioning is also that the Hague Conference on Private International Law, the governing body of the Hague Conventions, plays an important role in guiding

---

[107]   African Convention on Cybersecurity and Personal Data Protection, Art. 28.

the legal response to emerging issues in the area of international children's rights, such as international surrogacy.[108]

The relationship between the OPSC and the Hague Conventions, including the issue of international surrogacy, will be discussed in more detail in section 3.2.2.2.

2.7 ILO Convention No. 182, 1999

Another Convention explicitly mentioned in the preamble of the OPSC is the International Labour Organization Convention No. 182 on the Prohibition and Immediate Action for the Elimination of the Worst Forms of Child Labour (hereafter ILO Convention No. 182). In its Art 3, the Convention defines 'worst forms of child labour' as, inter alia, 'all forms of slavery or practices similar to slavery, such as the sale and trafficking of children' and 'the use of, procuring or offering of a child for prostitution, for the production of pornography or for pornographic performances'. The Convention provides for various prevention and response strategies to the worst forms of child labour, such as free basic education and direct assistance for the removal of children from the worst forms of child labour. In addition, Art 7 (1) of the Convention requires member states to take all necessary measures to ensure the effective implementation of the Convention, including the provision and application of penal sanctions. Considering that the Convention does not provide for a definition of any of the terms mentioned in Art 3, Art 2 and 3 OPSC should be considered *leges speciales* with regards to the criminalisation of sale of children, 'child prostitution' and 'child pornography'.

---

[108] For more details on the Parentage/Surrogacy project, see here: https://www.hcch.net/en/proj ects/legislative-projects/parentage-surrogacy (last accessed: 11 September 2021).

CHAPTER THREE

MEANING AND SCOPE

3.1 *Drafting History and Recent Developments*

The following section will provide a brief background on the drafting history of the OPSC and give an overview of the OPSC Guidelines and the CRC Committee's General Comment No. 25, which heavily influence today's interpretation and implementation of the OPSC.

3.1.1 *Drafting History of the OPSC*

As mentioned in Chapter One, the impetus for the development of the OPSC was born out of major concerns about the surge in commercial child sexual exploitation, and the impression that the CRC does not provide sufficient protection for child victims in such cases.

As much has been written about the discussions in the six working sessions which constitutes the drafting process of the OPSC,[109] this commentary will only focus on some of the highlights.

During the first session of the working group, the task was to come up with guidelines for a potential first draft OPSC. However, some members felt that the OPSC itself was not necessary and that the focus should be on the implementation of existing international standards, rather than focusing on a new instrument which might create contradictions and overlap with the existing standards. Supporters of the OPSC argued that there is indeed need for additional obligations which could complement the existing standards. This dispute continued in the second session, which—despite the ongoing debates—ended in the production of a first draft, which nonetheless was just a summary of the various proposals put forward during the second session. In the third session, the working group members finally overcame the divide and agreed that the OPSC would complement the CRC, and add considerable value by focusing on prevention, criminalising specific behaviours and international collaboration mechanisms. The fourth session finally allowed in-depth elaboration on the content of the OPSC, mainly the definition

---

[109] See Tobin, *The Optional Protocol on the Sale of Children, Child Prostitution, and Child Pornography*, pp. 1717 et seq.

© KONINKLIJKE BRILL NV, LEIDEN, 2022 | DOI:10.1163/9789004460393_004

of key terms such as 'sale of children', 'child prostitution' and 'child pornography'. It was debated whether the sale of children should only focus on aspects of sexual exploitation and whether 'child sex tourism' was absorbed under 'child prostitution' or 'child pornography', or whether a separate definition was required. Similar debates continued in the fifth session, which also involved a debate around the term 'unlawful' in the context of sexual activities, as discussed in section 2.1.4. Further, the need for universal jurisdiction and the extend of extradition agreements were debated. The session ended without clear consensus on any of the above topics, yet the Chairman remained positive that a final draft could be concluded in the sixth session of the protocol. Indeed, the Chairman of the Working Group produced a final draft during the sixth session which he believed reflected the minimum common basis of the deliberations. However, one contentious issue remained: the US wanted to become a state party to the OPSC, while not having ratified the UN CRC. While this was fiercely opposed by some members, the matter was finally settled by the Chairman's proposal to allow states who at least signed the CRC to also become States parties to the OPSC.

With this final stumbling block resolved, the final text of the OPSC was finally adopted by the UN General Assembly on 25 May 2000.[110]

3.1.2 Shaping Today's Interpretation of the OPSC

Even before the COVID-19 pandemic, it became clear that the impact of globalisation and digitalisation raised considerable challenges for the international community on how to prevent and respond to the sale and sexual exploitation of children. During the 2014 Day of General Discussion themed 'Digital media and children's rights', participants raised concerns that the CRC was adopted at a time when the Internet was still in its infancy. A digital-age specific interpretation of children's rights enshrined in the CRC was requested, either in the form of a new General Comment, a new Optional Protocol or even a new Convention.[111] The CRC Committee agreed with this view and came up with a two-pronged solution: the development of the Guidelines, adopted on 30 May 2019,[112] and the General

---

[110] For a detailed analysis of the working sessions, see Tobin, *The Optional Protocol on the Sale of Children, Child Prostitution, and Child Pornography*, pp. 1717 et seq.

[111] CRC Committee, *Report of the 2014 Day of General Discussion "Digital media and children's rights"*, Geneva 2014, available here: https://www.ohchr.org/Documents/HRBodies/CRC/Discussions/2014/DGD_report.pdf (last accessed: 1 December 2021).

[112] CRC Committee, *Guidelines regarding the implementation of the Optional Protocol to the Convention on the Rights of the Child on the sale of children, child prostitution and child pornography*, CRC/C/156.

Comment No. 25, adopted on 24 March 2021.[113] With these two instruments, the CRC Committee has given clear guidance on how it envisages the CRC and the OPSC to guide States parties through the complex challenges the protection of children from sale and sexual exploitation poses. A reoccurring theme within the interpretation of these documents will be how children's rights to privacy, expression, access to information and protection from all forms of violence, abuse and exploitation can be balanced without compromising one or the other.[114]

3.1.2.1 OPSC Guidelines

In the Guidelines, the CRC Committee recognises that '[w]hile the Convention and the Optional Protocol are fully relevant and applicable also in the digital environment, their provisions require an interpretation adapted to today's realities.'[115] The CRC Committee therefore aims 'to foster a deeper understanding of the Optional Protocol's substantive provisions and of the various modern forms of sale and sexual exploitation of children in light of developments in the digital environment and given the increase in knowledge and experience regarding the sale and sexual exploitation of children since its adoption.'[116]

As part of the general measures of implementation, the CRC Committee notes that any measure to implement the OPSC must comply with the CRC, stressing the need for age-appropriate child participation in the design and implementation of measures.[117] It highlights that specific consideration must be given to particularly vulnerable children 'including girls, boys, children of other gender or sex identities and orientations, children with disabilities, children in institutions, migrant children, children in street situations and children in other vulnerable or marginalised situation.'[118] The importance of highlighting both boys and girls as specifically vulnerable group, as well as the focus on LGBTIQ+ children, plays an important role throughout the interpretation of the OPSC as it impacts the design, implementation and evaluation of OPSC programmes.

---

[113] CRC Committee, *General comment No. 25 (2021) on children's rights in relation to the digital environment*, CRC/C/GC/25.

[114] Sonia Livingstone/Brian O'Neill, *Children's Rights Online. Challenges, Dilemmas and Emerging Directions* in: Simone van der Hof/Bibi van den Berg/Bart Schermer (eds.), *Minding Minors Wandering the Web: Regulating Online Child Safety*, The Hague 2014, p. 28.

[115] CRC Committee, *Guidelines regarding the implementation of the Optional Protocol to the Convention on the Rights of the Child on the sale of children, child prostitution and child pornography*, CRC/C/156, para. 1.

[116] Ibid., para. 9.

[117] Ibid., paras. 11–12.

[118] Ibid., para. 13; while this comprehensive list of grounds of discrimination is welcomed, it is noted that the CRC Committee throughout its Guidelines upholds the gender binary by speaking throughout of boys and girls only.

Continuing with the general measures of implementation, the Committee states the importance of developing and implementing comprehensive data collection, analysis, and dissemination frameworks, while ensuring that any form of data collection respects the child's right to privacy.[119] When developing a national comprehensive policy and strategy to address the issues covered by the OPSC, states are encouraged to include a variety of stakeholders such as 'financial institutions, bank, telecommunications operators, Internet providers, sports organizations, the travel and tourism industry and non-governmental organisation'.[120] Any activities related to the implementation of the OPSC should be closely coordinated cross-sectorally and on national, regional and local level. The implementation of policies and strategies should be regularly monitored and evaluated.[121] In order to ensure such activities are sufficiently funded, the Committee recommends that dedicated resources are made available through specific and clear budgetary allocations.[122]

Systematic, long-term, and in-depth awareness raising and information dissemination, including comprehensive sex education for children, are highlighted as important measures to enhance the understanding of the OPSC.[123] Lastly, the Committee states that training for all relevant professions, both multi-disciplinary and profession-specific, needs to be an integral part of the implementation of the OPSC. All trainings need to be based on victim-centred and survivor-led approaches and regularly assessed to ensure the acquired skills are indeed applied in practice.[124]

The OPSC Guidelines also provide insight into the legislation, national and transnational investigation as well as prevention measures considering the technological development since its adoption. These will be discussed in-depth within the sections of the specific articles below.

3.1.2.2 General Comment No. 25

In its General Comment No. 25, the CRC Committee acknowledges that '[t]he digital environment is becoming increasingly important across most aspects of children's lives, including during times of crisis, as societal functions, including education, government services and commerce, progressively come to rely upon

---

[119] CRC Committee, *General comment No. 25 (2021) on children's rights in relation to the digital environment*, CRC/C/GC/25), paras. 20–21.
[120] Ibid., paras. 22–23.
[121] Ibid., paras. 24–25.
[122] Ibid., para. 26.
[123] Ibid., para. 28.
[124] Ibid., para. 29.

digital technologies. It affords new opportunities for the realisation of children's rights, but also poses the risks of their violation and abuse.'[125] The Committee notes that the digital environment may open up new ways to perpetrate violence against children, such as live video-streaming or sexual extortion.[126] Forms of digitally facilitated violence might be perpetrated within a child's circle of trusts, and might include cyber aggressions such as bullying, but also promotion of self-harm such as suicidal behaviour or eating disorders.[127] Child exploitation may occur in various forms, such as economic exploitation, sexual exploitation and abuse, or the sale, trafficking or abduction of children.[128]

States are required to develop legislative and administrative measures to combat violence against children in the digital environment, including regular review and updating to ensure it addresses the latest emerging trends.[129] The CRC Committee hereby stresses that all safety and protective measures need to be in accordance with children's evolving capacities.[130] Surprisingly specific, the CRC Committee requires States parties to update anti-trafficking legislation to include technology-facilitated recruitment of children. It can be speculated that this specific reference is included as trafficking in children is not specifically covered by the OPSC Guidelines[131] and hence the opportunity was used to close the gap on a closely related offence and its interpretation in the context of the digital environment.

Even if legislation is in place to sanction child rights violations in the digital space, the difficulties in obtaining digital evidence, identifying perpetrators or the lack of knowledge on the side of children, parents and caregivers as to what constitutes a violation in the digital space might hinder children's access to justice.[132] Appropriate and effective judicial and non-judicial mechanisms should therefore be made widely known and be readily available.[133] These mechanisms should embrace multi-sectoral collaboration and make the avoidance of the child's revictimization the utmost priority.[134] As digital technologies bring additional complexities to the investigation and prosecution of crimes against children, specialised training should be provided to law enforcement officials, police and

---

[125] CRC Committee, *General comment No. 25 (2021) on children's rights in relation to the digital environment*, CRC/C/GC/25, para. 3.
[126] Ibid., para. 81.
[127] Ibid.
[128] Ibid., para. 112.
[129] Ibid., para. 82.
[130] Ibid., para. 82.
[131] For a discussion on the distinction between 'sale of children' and 'child trafficking', see section 3.2.2.2.
[132] Ibid., para. 43.
[133] Ibid., para. 44.
[134] Ibid., para. 45.

prosecution.[135] Considering the cross-border nature of the digital environment, the Committee recognises the need for strong international and regional cooperation, including the formulation of common definitions of criminal offences as well as strengthening mutual legal assistance mechanism and the joint collection and sharing of evidence.[136]

General Comment No. 25 plays an important role in complementing the OPSC Guidelines and draws connections to other children's rights and their interpretation in relation to the digital environment. It will be referenced more in-depth in relation to specific articles of the OPSC in the sections below.

3.2   Analysis of OPSC Articles

3.2.1   Art 1 OPSC: Prohibition

Article 1
States Parties shall prohibit the sale of children, child prostitution and child pornography as provided for by the present Protocol.

Art 1 makes it mandatory for States parties to prohibit the sale of children, 'child prostitution' and 'child pornography' as provided for by the OPSC. This means that States parties must cover the above offences by substantive criminal law,[137] not merely categorise them as administrative offences. This aims to recognise the above offences as severe child rights violations, which require the full force of the law as a response.

This requirement to 'prohibit' the above offences is in its wording more explicit than the obligations under Art 34–35 CRC. However, as it is acknowledged that the prohibition of such behaviour is an integral part of preventing and protecting children from the above harms and hence is already covered by the CRC, the question arises whether the OPSC is adding any relevant substantial content to the protection of children. Hereby it is important to notice that Art 1 needs to be read in conjunction with Art 2 and 3, which provide for a minimum standard for a definition of these terms as well as for a catalogue of offences. The advantage

---

[135] CRC Committee, *General comment No. 25 (2021) on children's rights in relation to the digital environment*, CRC/C/GC/25, para. 47.

[136] Ibid., paras. 123–124.

[137] CRC Committee, *Guidelines regarding the implementation of the Optional Protocol to the Convention on the Rights of the Child on the sale of children, child prostitution and child pornography*, CRC/C/156, para. 43.

of the OPSC is therefore its definitions and catalogue of offences which serve as clearly identified and easily monitorable goalposts for States parties.[138]

Further, Art 1 needs to be read in conjunction with Art 34 CRC, which broadly asks States parties to take all appropriate measures to prevent and respond to child abuse and exploitation. While prohibiting certain behaviour through criminal law is a key strategy, criminal law alone is insufficient to curb these offences due to its complexity and involvement of various stakeholders. In the context of the OPSC, additional legislative measures for professionals and the private sector, such as mandatory reporting of child sexual abuse materials for internet service providers, or the regulation of Artificial Intelligence to detect child sexual abuse material online, are areas which require broader legislative intervention and serve to complement the efforts of Art 1.

Art 1 hence sets the tone for the range of offences covered under the OPSC, which are further defined in Arts 2 and 3.

3.2.2 *Art 2 OPSC: Definitions*

Article 2
For the purposes of the present Protocol:
   (a) Sale of children means any act or transaction whereby a child is transferred by any person or group of persons to another for remuneration or any other consideration;
   (b) Child prostitution means the use of a child in sexual activities for remuneration or any other form of consideration;
   (c) Child pornography means any representation, by whatever means, of a child engaged in real or simulated explicit sexual activities or any representation of the sexual parts of a child for primarily sexual purposes.

3.2.2.1 Definitions: A Blessing and a Curse

Definitions in international treaties can be a blessing and a curse. A curse, because negotiations on their exact content might extensively prolong the drafting process or dilute their content. A blessing, because they might make the convention more easily implementable for States parties as the minimum scope of the obligations is clearly described.

---

[138] Tobin, *The Optional Protocol on the Sale of Children, Child Prostitution, and Child Pornography*, p. 1728.

While the debates about the definitions risked derailing the entire drafting process of the OPSC,[139] there is no doubt that Art 2 is one of the OPSC's strongest features which adds valuable weight in addition to Arts 34–36 CRC. However, some
of the definitions drafted during the negotiations of the OPSC in the 1990s have
not aged well and are at risk of failing today's protecting needs of children, which
will be discussed below.

3.2.2.2 'Sale of Children'

3.2.2.2.1 'Sale of Children'—an Overly Broad Definition?

The drafting of the definition of 'sale of children' solicited controversial debate
in the drafting process. The main issue was whether the 'sale of children' should
be limited to purposes of sexual exploitation, or whether also other purposes
should be considered such as in the case of child trafficking under the Palermo
Protocol.[140] Even though the focus of the OPSC was supposed to be on combatting commercial *sexual* exploitation of children, the definition of 'sale of children'
was rightfully extended beyond this narrow scope. An important argument was
that Art 35 CRC does not limit 'sale of children' in any way, hence a focus on sexual
exploitation would have led to a direct conflict between the OPSC and the CRC.[141]

Against this background, the definition of 'sale of children' can be split into two
components, firstly, 'any act or transaction whereby a child is transferred by any
person or group of persons to another' and secondly, 'for remuneration or any
other consideration'.

The term 'transfer' does neither specify the form of transfer nor the sending or
receiving parties. The parties could therefore be both known or unknown to the
child, and therefore also includes parents or legal guardians. Further, 'transfer'
does not necessarily require physical movement.[142] A 'transfer' of a child can
also be performed if the actual authority over a child, whether in form of legal
guardianship or simply actual supervisory power, is transferred from one person to another. This is for example the case if a guardian, who leaves the country to look for a job abroad, leaves the child at home with the extended family

---

[139] Tobin, *The Optional Protocol on the Sale of Children, Child Prostitution, and Child Pornography*,
p. 1729.
[140] UNICEF Innocenti, *Handbook on the Optional Protocol on the Sale of Children, Child
Prostitution and Child Pornography*, p. 9.
[141] Vandenhole/Türkelli/Lembrechts, *Children's Rights. A Commentary on the Rights of the Child
and its Optional Protocol*, p. 447; Tobin, *The Optional Protocol on the Sale of Children, Child Prostitution,
and Child Pornography*, p. 1730.
[142] UNICEF Innocenti, *Handbook on the Optional Protocol on the Sale of Children, Child
Prostitution and Child Pornography*, p. 10.

who provide shelter to the child, but the child is in return forced to participate in hazardous labour. In such a situation, the child has not physically moved, yet the actual authority over the child was transferred.

The second element is the 'remuneration or any other consideration'. The CRC Committee stresses that even though this usually involves some form of payment, also other forms of consideration fall under the definition, such as 'payment of a debt by the parents, a promise by the other person that the child will receive education or vocational training, or other kinds of offer for a better future'.[143] This broad scope needs to be critically reflected against the background that transferring a child to a third party, for example teachers or caretakers, poses an everyday event in a child's life. However, one would not categorise such 'transfer' as 'sale of children' as there might be no clear remuneration for the transfer. However, the line gets blurrier if we look at the common practice of sending children from their rural homes to (often distant) relatives in the urban areas or abroad, so the children can receive a (better) education. Looking closely at the element of 'remuneration', one could argue that the parents are only sending the child away for a better education to improve their chances of being taken care of once they are elderly. This would pose an advancement of the transferor's lifestyle and hence be considered 'sale of children'. For the careful reader, this does not seem to be right. We might feel like the parents have the child's best interests at heart, and if in the long run they also benefit from the transfer, then this is just a side effect but not the main purpose of the transfer. So, is it only 'sale of children' if the benefit is received instantly? Or is it rather relevant that the 'consideration' which the transferor receives is considered an 'improper' benefit? The CRC Committee does not take a stance on this matter in its Guidelines. However, reading this additional element into the definition would certainly shield parents from being criminalised for a transfer which to a certain degree also benefits themselves, but primarily aims to improve the child's prospects.

This shows that the broadness of the definition of 'sale of children', even though drafted with the aim to avoid any legal gaps, might prove to be too far reaching in some circumstances. Other situations where the broadness of the definition poses challenges is the area of surrogacy as well as 'voluntourism' and orphanage tourism, which will be discussed below.

---

[143] CRC Committee, *Guidelines regarding the implementation of the Optional Protocol to the Convention on the Rights of the Child on the sale of children, child prostitution and child pornography,* CRC/C/156, para. 46.

3.2.2.2.2 Sale of Children and Child Trafficking

One of the major challenges regarding the 'sale of children' is the wrongful perception that it is identical with child trafficking. While these criminal offences can overlap, it is important to note that the legal definitions differ.[144] Child trafficking is defined in Art 3 (c) Palermo Protocol as 'recruitment, transportation, transfer, harbouring or receipt of a child for the purpose of exploitation'. Notably, none of the means usually required for trafficking, such as coercion, deception or abuse of power needs to be present for a case of child trafficking, as a child cannot consent to its own exploitation.[145]

The CRC Committee in the OPSC Guidelines highlights that 'sale of children' always requires some form of commercial transaction ('remuneration or other consideration'), which is not required for child trafficking.[146] On the other hand, child trafficking needs to pursue an exploitative purpose. If States parties wrongfully assume that an exploitative purpose is required for a sale of children charge, this might potentially weaken such a case as an exploitative purpose is in fact not required by law and hence does not need to be proven.[147] An additional difference is that sale of children, as discussed above, does not require the physical transfer of a child. In contrast, removing a child out of their social environment is a key element of child trafficking and the reason why trafficked children are particularly vulnerable.[148] Despite the above differences, it cannot be denied that in practice there is often an overlap of these offences.[149] This should not stop States parties from acknowledging that these offences are separate in nature and hence require different criminal provisions.

However, most States parties do not follow this distinction and use the terms 'sale of children' and 'child trafficking' interchangeably, although Art 35 CRC also describes them as different concepts. It is therefore a common concluding

---

[144] CRC Committee, *Guidelines regarding the implementation of the Optional Protocol to the Convention on the Rights of the Child on the sale of children, child prostitution and child pornography*, CRC/C/156, para. 49.

[145] See wording of Art 3 (c) Palermo Protocol: 'even if this does not involve any of the means set forth in subparagraph (a) of this article'.

[146] CRC Committee, *Guidelines regarding the implementation of the Optional Protocol to the Convention on the Rights of the Child on the sale of children, child prostitution and child pornography*, CRC/C/156, para. 15.

[147] ECPAT, *Explanatory Report to the Guidelines Regarding the Implementation of the Optional Protocol to the Convention on the Rights of the Child on the Sale of Children, Child Prostitution and Child Pornography*, p. 25.

[148] UNICEF Innocenti, *Handbook on the Optional Protocol on the Sale of Children, Child Prostitution and Child Pornography*, p. 10.

[149] CRC Committee, *Guidelines regarding the implementation of the Optional Protocol to the Convention on the Rights of the Child on the sale of children, child prostitution and child pornography*, CRC/C/156, para. 15.

observation for State party reports on the OPSC to include a reminder for States parties to criminalise 'sale of children' and 'child trafficking' as separate offences.[150] Lastly, the CRC Committee requires States parties to ensure that their child trafficking legislation also includes technology-facilitated recruitment.[151]

3.2.2.2.3 Commercial and Altruistic Surrogacy

The sale of children in the context of surrogacy is a complex, highly political and strongly debated issue. Surrogacy describes the practice where intending parent(s) and the surrogate mother agree that the surrogate mother will become pregnant, gestate and give birth to a child.[152] The practice has been starkly increasing since the early 2000s, which can be attributed to scientific developments such as artificial insemination and in-vitro fertilisation, increasing infertility rates in some parts of the world and the growing acceptance of 'alternative' family forms.[153]

There are various forms of surrogacy which trigger complex children's and women's rights questions. Firstly, there is a distinction between traditional and gestational surrogacy, whereby the mother is genetically related to the child in cases of traditional surrogacy and genetically unrelated in cases of gestational surrogacy. Further, there is an important difference between commercial and altruistic surrogacy. In cases of altruistic surrogacy, the intending parent(s) pay the surrogate mother only for her 'reasonable expenses' related to the surrogacy. In the case of commercial surrogacy, the intending parent(s) pay the surrogate a financial remuneration which goes beyond the 'reasonable expenses', such as a payment

---

[150] Committee on the Rights of the Child, *Concluding observations on the report submitted by Angola under article 12 (1) of the Optional Protocol to the Convention on the Rights of the Child on the sale of children, child prostitution and child pornography*, CRC/C/OPSC/AGO/CO/1 (29 June 2018), para. 25; Committee on the Rights of the Child, *Concluding observations on the report submitted by Czechia under article 12 (1) of the Optional Protocol to the Convention on the Rights of the Child on the sale of children, child prostitution and child pornography*, CRC/C/OPSC/CZE/CO/1 (5 March 2019), para. 9; Committee on the Rights of the Child, *Concluding observations on the report submitted by Georgia under article 12 (1) of the Optional Protocol to the Convention on the Rights of the Child on the sale of children, child prostitution and child pornography*, CRC/C/OPSC/GEO/CO/1 (30 October 2019), para. 29; Committee on the Rights of the Child, *Concluding observations on the report submitted by Tajikistan under article 12 (1) of the Optional Protocol to the Convention on the Rights of the Child on the sale of children, child prostitution and child pornography*, CRC/C/OPSC/TJK/CO/1 (3 November 2017), para. 27.

[151] CRC Committee, *General comment No. 25 (2021) on children's rights in relation to the digital environment*, CRC/C/GC/25, para. 115.

[152] Maud de Boer-Buquiccio, *Report of the Special Rapporteur on the sale and sexual exploitation of children, including child prostitution, child pornography and other child sexual abuse material*, A/HRC/37/60 (15 January 2018), para. 10.

[153] Hague Conference on Private International Law, *A preliminary report on the issues arising from international surrogacy arrangements*, The Hague 2012, pp. 6–7.

to compensate for pain and suffering or simply a fee which the surrogate mother charges.[154]

To ensure that the interests and rights of the various stakeholders are protected and balanced, international and national legal frameworks play a key role. However, the regulation of surrogacy in national laws varies considerably, from non-existent to extensive, and from liberal to prohibitive. Some countries only permit altruistic surrogacy, allow for commercial surrogacy only under specific circumstances or flat-out prohibit all forms of surrogacy.[155] This inconsistency across States parties often leads to a situation in which national courts need to validate international surrogacy agreements which are illegal in at least one involved state. This requires the courts to balance the child's rights to identity and nationality with the intending parent(s) interests and the surrogate mother's rights.[156] Vulnerabilities affecting surrogate mothers are a reality in the surrogacy business, with many intending parent(s) from the Global North approaching surrogate mothers in the Global South who can be vulnerable to exploitation due to poverty, lack of education and intersecting forms of discrimination.[157] A particularly daunting role is played by intermediaries, which see surrogacy as a for-profit business with children as mere commodities.[158] However, while considering these vulnerabilities, it is also important to not automatically deprive women of agency in making their own decisions on this matter, as this reiterates the harmful gender stereotype of women's innate role as 'selfless mothers'.[159]

The main question in the context of the OPSC is whether surrogacy, in particular commercial surrogacy, amounts to the sale of children and is hence a prohibited practice under the OPSC. The CRC Committee in its Guidelines avoids a concrete decision on this subject matter, and merely 'encourages States parties in which this practice exists to take all necessary measures, including regulation, to avoid the

---

[154] Hague Conference on Private International Law, *A preliminary report on the issues arising from international surrogacy arrangements*, The Hague 2012, Annex p. i.

[155] de Boer-Buquicchio, *Report of the Special Rapporteur on the sale and sexual exploitation of children, including child prostitution, child pornography and other child sexual abuse material*, A/HRC/37/60, para. 15.

[156] Ibid., para. 17.

[157] Ibid.

[158] ECPAT, *Explanatory Report to the Guidelines Regarding the Implementation of the Optional Protocol to the Convention on the Rights of the Child on the Sale of Children, Child Prostitution and Child Pornography*, p. 60.

[159] Center for Reproductive Rights, *Submission from the Center for Reproductive Rights following the call for inputs by the Special Rapporteur on the Sale and Sexual Exploitation of Children on Safeguards for the protection of the rights of children born from surrogate arrangements*, New York (undated), p. 6.

sale of children under surrogacy arrangements.'[160] At a minimum, this indicates that surrogacy *can*, but does not have to constitute sale of children in the opinion of the CRC Committee.[161] The Special Rapporteur in her 2018 report fleshed out this position in considerable detail, essentially arguing that commercial surrogacy could be conducted in a way that does not constitute the sale of children. This would however depend on the application of very strict conditions pertaining to—inter alia—the status of the mother at birth, the payment conditions and role of intermediaries, paired with a mandatory post-birth individualised best interests assessment.[162] Similarly, the Special Rapporteur concludes that altruistic surrogacy does not necessarily amount to the sale of children, if it is comprehensively regulated by for example requiring that all payments to the surrogate mother are reasonable and itemised and subject to judicial oversight.[163]

While clear international standards are missing and national legislation is inconsistent, the Special Rapporteur asks states to neither automatically accept nor reject (partly) illegal surrogacy arrangements.[164] Instead of insisting on setting an example by banking on the deterrent effect of the rejection of illegal surrogacy arrangements, states should always put the best interests of the child first and assess each situation on an individual basis.

3.2.2.2.4 Sale of Children in the Context of Sports

Children's rights in the context of sports are violated as a direct result of their participation in sports or at the margins of major sports events.[165] There are several scenarios which can amount to the sale of children as defined in the OPSC. Firstly, many child athletes do not have a written contract or if they have one, they do not have a copy readily available, which makes them vulnerable to various forms of exploitation.[166] Children are at further risk of exploitation and abuse in the context of third-party ownerships, whereby a third party such as a business or an

---

[160] CRC Committee, *Guidelines regarding the implementation of the Optional Protocol to the Convention on the Rights of the Child on the sale of children, child prostitution and child pornography*, CRC/C/156, para. 52.

[161] Ibid.

[162] de Boer-Buquiccio, *Report of the Special Rapporteur on the sale and sexual exploitation of children, including child prostitution, child pornography and other child sexual abuse material*, A/HRC/37/60, paras. 72 et seq.

[163] Ibid., para. 76.

[164] Maud de Boer-Buquiccio, *Report of the Special Rapporteur on the sale and sexual exploitation of children, including child prostitution, child pornography and other child sexual abuse material*, A/74/162 (15 July 2019), para. 91.

[165] Maud de Boer-Buquiccio, *Report of the special rapporteur on the sale and sexual exploitation of children, including child prostitution, child pornography and other child sexual abuse material*, A/HRC/40/51 (27 December 2018), para. 13.

[166] Ibid., para. 52.

investment fund partly owns the 'economic rights' of players. This commodifies the player and especially in relation to child athletes, can lead to a relationship of ownership with the third parties.[167] Children from the Global South are particularly vulnerable to transfers to sports academies in the Global North, which scout young talent to train them to professional athletes' level. Children are put under extreme pressure, have little contact with their families and lack decision-making powers over their career.[168] Lastly, beneath practices of sale of children, child trafficking also plays a major role in the context of sports, with children being majority of trafficking victims in professional football.[169] As an example, children from poor families in low-income countries who aspire to become professional footballers are trafficked into Europe.[170] Considering the opportunities athletic excellence offers to children from the Global South to receive scholarships and sponsorships, they are particularly vulnerable to become victims of sale or sexual exploitation.[171]

Children are further at high risk of sexual abuse in the sports environment, with young children being particularly vulnerable.[172] Grooming plays an important role. Considering the close relationship that develops between child athletes and coaches, trainers and medical personnel, professional sports create an environment in which grooming might be difficult to recognise for the victim and others.[173] The power dynamics present between children and their adult trainers and coaches and the often authoritative style of elite sports render children particularly vulnerable and might stop them from speaking up.[174] Sports organisations interests to preserve their image also played a considerable role in one the world's biggest sexual abuse cases in relation to sports, the abuse of hundreds of girls and women through the US women's gymnastics team's former team doctor.[175] During Senate hearings, elite gymnast and sexual abuse survivor Simone Biles clearly put

---

[167] Maud de Boer-Buquiccio, *Report of the special rapporteur on the sale and sexual exploitation of children, including child prostitution, child pornography and other child sexual abuse material*, A/HRC/40/51 (27 December 2018), para. 60.

[168] Ibid., para. 63.

[169] Ibid., para. 68.

[170] UNICEF Innocenti, *The sale and sexual exploitation of children in the context of sport and sporting events*, Florence 2020, p. 1.

[171] Ibid., p. 2.

[172] ECPAT, *Explanatory Report to the Guidelines Regarding the Implementation of the Optional Protocol to the Convention on the Rights of the Child on the Sale of Children, Child Prostitution and Child Pornography*, p. 12.

[173] Ibid., p. 71.

[174] de Boer-Buquiccio, *Report of the special rapporteur on the sale and sexual exploitation of children, including child prostitution, child pornography and other child sexual abuse material*, A/HRC/40/51, para. 72.

[175] Ibid., para. 74.

responsibility not only on the team doctor as an individual, but on the 'entire system that enabled and perpetrated her abuse'.[176]

In the same vein, the CRC Committee encourages States parties to pay increased attention to the role of sports organisations, and to use the Guiding Principles on Business and Human Rights framework to protect children's rights in the context of sports.[177] This framework regulates that business have the responsibility to respect human rights by undertaking human rights due diligence, ergo identifying, preventing, mitigating and accounting for human rights violations.[178] These principles are hereby of direct relevance for the sports industry, including sport governing bodies.[179] The liability of both natural and legal persons is regulated in Art 3 (4) and sports organisations are therefore not exempted from liability in cases of child rights violations.[180]

3.2.2.2.5   Child Marriages

The CRC Committee in its Guidelines stresses that the sale of children can also occur in the context of child marriages, recommending States parties to take all necessary measures to avoid the sale of children in this context.[181] The CRC and the CEDAW Committees in their joint General Comment No. 31 (2014) define child marriage as 'any marriage where at least one of the parties is under 18 years of age'. Child marriages are considered a form of forced marriages, as at least one party has not expressed their full, free and informed consent.[182] However, General

---

[176] BBC News, *Simone Biles: 'I blame system that enabled Larry Nassar abuse'*, 15 September 2021, available here: https://www.bbc.com/news/world-us-canada-58573887 (last accessed: 2 October 2021).

[177] CRC Committee, *Guidelines regarding the implementation of the Optional Protocol to the Convention on the Rights of the Child on the sale of children, child prostitution and child pornography*, CRC/C/156, para. 23.

[178] de Boer-Buquiccio, *Report of the special rapporteur on the sale and sexual exploitation of children, including child prostitution, child pornography and other child sexual abuse material*, A/HRC/40/51, para. 28.

[179] ECPAT, *Explanatory Report to the Guidelines Regarding the Implementation of the Optional Protocol to the Convention on the Rights of the Child on the Sale of Children, Child Prostitution and Child Pornography*, p. 35.

[180] de Boer-Buquiccio, *Report of the special rapporteur on the sale and sexual exploitation of children, including child prostitution, child pornography and other child sexual abuse material*, A/HRC/40/51, para. 24.

[181] CRC Committee, *Guidelines regarding the implementation of the Optional Protocol to the Convention on the Rights of the Child on the sale of children, child prostitution and child pornography*, CRC/C/156, para. 51.

[182] CEDAW Committee/CRC Committee, *Joint general recommendation/general comment No. 31 of the Committee on the Elimination of Discrimination against Women and No. 18 of the Committee on the Rights of the Child on harmful practices*, CEDAW/C/GC31-CRC/C/GC/18 (4 November 2014), para. 20; for an in-depth discussion on the terms 'child marriage', 'early marriage' and 'forced marriage' see ECPAT, *Terminology Guidelines for the Protection of Children from Sexual Exploitation and Sexual Abuse*, pp. 63 et seq.

Comment No. 31 (2014) sets out that under exceptional circumstances and after approval by a judge, a child might be deemed mature enough at the age of 16 years to enter into marriage, taking into account the child's evolving capacity and autonomy.[183] This exception was abolished in the 2019 version of joint General Comment No. 31 without any further explanation, setting an absolute age of marriage at 18 years.[184]

Child marriages often include a financial transaction such as the payment of a dowry or a bride price. Further, parents may give their daughters temporarily to a husband in exchange for financial gain. Handing over a daughter into marriage might also be used to settle family debts or provide for economic security.[185] The CRC Committee has identified the practice of *wahayu* or fifth wives, in which the girls are treated as property and economically and sexually exploited, as a form of sale of children.[186] Where such a financial transaction is involved, the child marriage might amount to the sale of children as defined in Art 2.[187]

3.2.2.3 'Child Prostitution'

3.2.2.3.1 Terminology and Conceptualisation
Art 2 (b) defines 'child prostitution' as 'the use of a child in sexual activities for remuneration or any other form of consideration'. Firstly, the CRC Committee follows the recommendation in the Luxembourg Guidelines to move away from the term 'child prostitution', as it creates the connotation that the child voluntarily participates and might be misunderstood to shift the blame onto the

---

[183] CEDAW Committee/CRC Committee, *Joint general recommendation/general comment No. 31 of the Committee on the Elimination of Discrimination against Women and No. 18 of the Committee on the Rights of the Child on harmful practices*, CEDAW/C/GC31-CRC/C/GC/18, para. 19; in contrast to the CEDAW and CRC Committee, the African children's rights framework does not allow for such an exception and sets the age of consent to marriage at 18 years, see African Union Commission, *Joint general comment of the African Commission on Human and People's Rights and the African Committee of Experts on the Rights and Welfare of the Child on ending child marriages*, Addis Ababa 2017, p. 6.

[184] CEDAW Committee/CRC Committee, *Joint general recommendation/general comment No. 31 of the Committee on the Elimination of Discrimination against Women and No. 18 of the Committee on the Rights of the Child (2019) on harmful practices*, CEDAW/C/GC31/Rev.1-CRC/C/GC/18/Rev.1, para. 20 et seq.

[185] Najat Maalla M'jid, *Report of the Special Rapporteur on the sale of children, child prostitution and child pornography*, A/HRC/25/48 (23 December 2013), para. 26.

[186] CRC Committee, *Concluding observations on the report submitted by Niger under article 12 (1) of the Optional Protocol to the Convention on the Rights of the Child on the sale of children, child prostitution and child pornography*, CRC/C/OPSC/NER/CO/1 (12 December 2018), para. 19.

[187] CEDAW Committee/CRC Committee, *Joint general recommendation/general comment No. 31 of the Committee on the Elimination of Discrimination against Women and No. 18 f the Committee on the Rights of the Child (2019) on harmful practices*, CEDAW/C/GC31/Rev.1-CRC/C/GC/18/Ref.1, para. 24.

child.[188] However, it needs to be stressed that children cannot consent to their own exploitation[189] and should also not be held criminally liable in any way.[190] Therefore, the CRC Committee endorses the terms 'children who are prostituted' or 'children who are exploited in prostitution'.[191] Considering that the latter is similar to the formulation used in Art 34 CRC ('the exploitative use of children in prostitution'),[192] this is the term which will be used in this commentary.

The CRC Committee defines the term 'sexual activities' to include 'at a minimum and whether real or simulated, all forms of sexual intercourse and intentional sexual touching involving a child, independent of the sex of all involved persons, and any lascivious exhibition of the genitals or the pubic area of a child'.[193] As the term 'sexual activities' is not closer defined in the OPSC, this additional definition is indeed helpful for the drafting of national legislation. It is important to note that the definition does not require penetration and is also gender-neutral, hence every person can be perpetrator or victim.[194]

As for the second element of the definition, 'for remuneration or any other consideration', this element must be interpreted broadly and include not only financial gains but also provision of food, shelter or any other form of basic survival support.[195] The benefit does not even have to materialise, the mere promise of remuneration or other consideration suffices to fulfil this element of the definition.[196] Further, it is not required that the child is the one which benefits

---

[188] CRC Committee, *Guidelines regarding the implementation of the Optional Protocol to the Convention on the Rights of the Child on the sale of children, child prostitution and child pornography*, CRC/C/156, paras. 5, 55.

[189] Ibid., para. 54.

[190] ECPAT, *Explanatory Report to the Guidelines Regarding the Implementation of the Optional Protocol to the Convention on the Rights of the Child on the Sale of Children, Child Prostitution and Child Pornography*, p. 62.

[191] CRC Committee, *Guidelines regarding the implementation of the Optional Protocol to the Convention on the Rights of the Child on the sale of children, child prostitution and child pornography*, CRC/C/156, para. 59, in line with ECPAT, *Terminology Guidelines for the Protection of Children from Sexual Exploitation and Sexual Abuse*, p. 30.

[192] ECPAT, *Explanatory Report to the Guidelines Regarding the Implementation of the Optional Protocol to the Convention on the Rights of the Child on the Sale of Children, Child Prostitution and Child Pornography*, p. 62.

[193] CRC Committee, *Guidelines regarding the implementation of the Optional Protocol to the Convention on the Rights of the Child on the sale of children, child prostitution and child pornography*, CRC/C/156, para. 53.

[194] ECPAT, *Explanatory Report to the Guidelines Regarding the Implementation of the Optional Protocol to the Convention on the Rights of the Child on the Sale of Children, Child Prostitution and Child Pornography*, p. 61.

[195] CRC Committee, *Guidelines regarding the implementation of the Optional Protocol to the Convention on the Rights of the Child on the sale of children, child prostitution and child pornography*, CRC/C/156, para. 54.

[196] Ibid., para. 56.

from the remuneration or other consideration, this could also be a third party.[197] Even if the child is the one benefitting from the remuneration, it is important to note that this still constitutes sexual exploitation and hence a criminal offence.[198]

Further, the CRC Committee notes that sexual exploitation of children in prostitution also occurs in 'commodified' relationships, in which sexual acts are exchanged for cash, goods or benefits, often linked to economic survival or opportunities, educational achievement or social status'.[199] To describe this constellation, the previously accepted term 'transactional sex' should be avoided as it might be understood to legitimise a form of sexual exploitation, which is built on an imbalance of power. This power is used 'by an adult to coerce, entice, or compel a child into engaging in sexual activities' and should hence be called what it actually is: sexual exploitation.[200] Children in street situations, children on the move and children affected by humanitarian crises are at particular risk of being exploited in the context of 'commodified' relationships.[201] Acknowledging the grave child rights violations, such as child sexual exploitation, committed by peacekeeping forces and international humanitarian personnel, immediate preventative and response action is required to ensure that the people who are supposed to protect civilians do not exploit their vulnerabilities.[202]

3.2.2.3.2 Online Exploitation of Children in Prostitution

In its Guidelines, the CRC Committee recognises that children are also exploited for prostitution online, for example by advertising children for sexual activity through websites or mobile applications. Therefore, the Committee urges States parties to ensure that their legislation also applies to the exploitative use

---

[197] ECPAT, *Explanatory Report to the Guidelines Regarding the Implementation of the Optional Protocol to the Convention on the Rights of the Child on the Sale of Children, Child Prostitution and Child Pornography*, p. 62.

[198] Ibid.

[199] CRC Committee, *Guidelines regarding the implementation of the Optional Protocol to the Convention on the Rights of the Child on the sale of children, child prostitution and child pornography*, CRC/C/156, para. 58.

[200] ECPAT, *Terminology Guidelines for the Protection of Children from Sexual Exploitation and Sexual Abuse*, pp. 33 et seq.

[201] ECPAT, *Explanatory Report to the Guidelines Regarding the Implementation of the Optional Protocol to the Convention on the Rights of the Child on the Sale of Children, Child Prostitution and Child Pornography*, p. 64; de Boer-Buquiccio/ Giammarinaro, *Joint report of the Special Rapporteur on the sale and sexual exploitation of children, including child prostitution, child pornography and other child sexual abuse material and the Special Rapporteur on trafficking in persons, especially women and children*, A/72/164, paras. 28 et seq.

[202] de Boer-Buquiccio/ Giammarinaro, *Joint report of the Special Rapporteur on the sale and sexual exploitation of children, including child prostitution, child pornography and other child sexual abuse material and the Special Rapporteur on trafficking in persons, especially women and children*, A/72/164, paras. 28 et seq.

of children in prostitution through the use of ICT.[203] Such exploitative practices may increase due to poverty caused by COVID-19. In the Philippines, authorities discovered that teenagers share their sexual material online to fund expenses in online learning.[204]

Recently, the online exploitation of children in prostitution was debated in the context of the platform OnlyFans. OnlyFans, a subscriber-only website, is most well-known for it's pornographic content and has exploded in popularity in 2020 as sex work—like many professions—moved online amid the COVID-19 pandemic.[205] However, reports revealed that also children create and share pornographic material of themselves on OnlyFans. A common theme emerged among multiple cases: children are enticed by the promise of easy money, as well as the hope of growing in popularity and social influence.[206]

Circling back to the discussion on Art 34 ('*exploitative* use of children in prostitution'), the question arises whether all these cases should be automatically categorized as exploitative 'child prostitution' or whether some of this behavior might be considered non-exploitative. The CRC Committee is clear that whenever there is a commercial element involved, the child cannot consent under any circumstances and the conduct will not be protected under Art 16 CRC as form of sexual exploration/expression. Even though this is not explicitly mentioned in the Guidelines, the CRC Committee indirectly endorses this approach by not mentioning any possible exemptions to the welfarist approach pursued by the OPSC in contrast to Art 34 CRC. As the CRC Committee makes very narrow exemptions for certain categories of pornographic images of children (discussed in section 3.2.2.4) which are created without 'remuneration or any other consideration' under the definition of 'child pornography', it is clear that the lack of an exemption for similar constellations under the 'child prostitution' offence was a deliberate decision.

In conclusion, any form of children's exploitative use in prostitution, both online and offline, is prohibited under the OPSC.

---

[203] CRC Committee, *Guidelines regarding the implementation of the Optional Protocol to the Convention on the Rights of the Child on the sale of children, child prostitution and child pornography*, CRC/C/156, para. 57.

[204] WeProtect Global Alliance, *Global Threat Assessment 2021*, p. 57.

[205] Kari Paul, *OnlyFans ban on sexually explicit content will endanger lives, say US sex workers*, The Guardian (20 August 2021), available here: https://www.theguardian.com/us-news/2021/aug/20/onlyfans-ban-porn-sexually-explicit-content-risk-lives-sex-workers (last accessed: 5 October 2021).

[206] Noel Titheradge/Rianna Croxford, *The children selling explicit videos on OnlyFans*, BBC (27 May 2021), available here: https://www.bbc.com/news/uk-57255983 (last accessed: 5 October 2021).

3.2.2.3.3   Sexual Exploitation of Children in Travel and Tourism

The sexual exploitation of children in travel and tourism (hereafter: SECTT) is one of the contexts in which many offences contained in the OPSC occur. Considering this, SECTT could have also been discussed in the context of any other offence in the OPSC: the subsummation under 'child prostitution' merely follows the structure of the OPSC Guidelines, in which the regulation of SECTT is discussed in the context of 'child prostitution'.[207]

As has been mentioned in the drafting history, the concern about sexual exploitation in the travel and tourism sector was one of the driving factors for the development of the OPSC. Against this background, it is somewhat surprising that the sexual exploitation of children in travel and tourism ('child sex tourism') is only mentioned twice in the OPSC: in the preamble and in the context of Art 10 CRC (international cooperation). It is not included as a separate offence in Arts 2 or 3. As a starting point, it must be acknowledged that the CRC Committee, in line with the Luxembourg Guidelines, moved away from the term 'child sex tourism' as it might give the idea that this constitutes a legitimate form of tourism. The commonly used term is 'sexual exploitation of children in travel and tourism' (common abbreviation is SECTT).[208]

Before the CRC Committee issued its guidelines in 2019, the Committee required States parties to develop a separate criminal law provision on SECTT as can be seen in multiple pre-Guidelines concluding observations.[209] This poses the question what the added advantage of such a specific provision would be. From a legal perspective, if the various forms of exploitation are already sufficiently covered in the criminal law (despite not making specific reference to the travel and tourism

---

[207] CRC Committee, *Guidelines regarding the implementation of the Optional Protocol to the Convention on the Rights of the Child on the sale of children, child prostitution and child pornography*, CRC/C/156, para. 59; ECPAT, *Terminology Guidelines for the Protection of Children from Sexual Exploitation and Sexual Abuse*, p. 59.

[208] ECPAT, *Terminology Guidelines for the Protection of Children from Sexual Exploitation and Sexual Abuse*, p. 56.

[209] See selection of concluding observations which were issued before the Guidelines were adopted on 10 September 2019, CRC Committee, *Concluding observations on the report submitted by Angola under article 12 (1) of the Optional Protocol to the Convention on the Rights of the Child on the sale of children, child prostitution and child pornography*, CRC/C/OPSC/AGO/CO/1, para. 26; CRC Committee, *Concluding observations on the report submitted by Benin under article 12 (1) of the Optional Protocol to the Convention on the Rights of the Child on the sale of children, child prostitution and child pornography*, CRC/C/OPSC/BEN/CO/1 (29 November 2018), para. 25; CRC Committee, *Concluding observations on the report submitted by Czechia under article 12 (1) of the Optional Protocol to the Convention on the Rights of the Child on the sale of children, child prostitution and child pornography*, CRC/C/OPSC/CZE/CO/1, para. 10; Committee on the Rights of the Child, *Concluding observations on the report submitted by Saudi Arabia under article 12 (1) of the Optional Protocol to the Convention on the Rights of the Child on the sale of children, child prostitution and child pornography*, CRC/C/OPSC/SAU/CO/1 (31 October 2018), para. 23.

sector), there is no legal gap which requires closing. As a comparison, the problem of sexual exploitation of children in the context of sports has been widely emphasised by the CRC Committee, yet there was not a call for a separate criminal offence for that context. Rather, the Committee stressed that context-specific prevention and response mechanisms must be established.

Since the adoption of the OPSC Guidelines in 2019, the CRC Committee seems to have followed this approach as it does not require a separate offence for SECTT anymore. Instead, the CRC Committee suggests that 'sexual exploitation of children in travel and tourism [...] is included in the offences covered by the Optional Protocol'.[210] Even though Art 1 does not make specific reference to this, the sale of children, 'child prostitution' and 'child pornography' often occur in the context of travel and tourism and are hence covered by the provision of Art 1, as long as one of the specifically mentioned criminal offences takes place in this context.[211] Sexual exploitation of children in travel and tourism should hence not be considered a standalone criminal offence, but rather a sector in which the offences laid out in Art 1 often occur and which hence requires States parties and the travel and tourism sector to take specific measures.[212]

When discussing SECTT, the meaning and scope have considerably evolved over the years. While it was initially understood to typically include international travel, the CRC Committee made it clear that 'offenders may be foreign or domestic tourists and travellers or long-term visitors'.[213] This change in scope has been prompted by research which showed SECTT is now mainly a domestic and intra-regional crime which can be found in most developed and least developed

---

[210] CRC Committee, *Guidelines regarding the implementation of the Optional Protocol to the Convention on the Rights of the Child on the sale of children, child prostitution and child pornography*, CRC/C/156, para. 59.

[211] Stating that sex tourism involving children is directly linked to the offences covered by the Optional Protocol, Najat Maalla M'jid, *Report of the Special Rapporteur on the sale of children, child prostitution and child pornography*, A/HRC/22/54 (24 December 2012), para. 42.

[212] ECPAT, *Explanatory Report to the Guidelines Regarding the Implementation of the Optional Protocol to the Convention on the Rights of the Child on the Sale of Children, Child Prostitution and Child Pornography*, p. 65; however, one could think of requesting States parties to criminalise offences related to the business of child sexual exploitation in tourism and travel, such as the criminalisation of advertisement of children for sexual activity in this sector under South African law, see Committee on the Rights of the Child, *Concluding observations on the report submitted by South Africa under article 12 (1) of the Optional Protocol to the Convention on the Rights of the Child on the sale of children, child prostitution and child pornography*, CRC/C/OPSC/ZAF/CO/1 (26 October 2016), para. 24. This would indeed add additional value to the criminal framework and assist in combatting child exploitation specifically in the context of travel and tourism.

[213] CRC Committee, *Guidelines regarding the implementation of the Optional Protocol to the Convention on the Rights of the Child on the sale of children, child prostitution and child pornography*, CRC/C/156 (10 September 2019), para. 59; ECPAT, *Terminology Guidelines for the Protection of Children from Sexual Exploitation and Sexual Abuse*, p. 55.

countries.[214] In order to successfully combat SECTT, extraterritorial jurisdiction plays an important role. However, transnational investigation is complex and time-consuming, hence hampering countries to effectively prosecute transnational offenders.[215] Systematic exchange of information between law enforcement agencies is required to prevent convicted offenders from reoffending in other countries.[216]

3.2.2.3.4 'Voluntourism' and 'Orphanage Tourism'

Another practice which requires attention is the increase in so-called 'voluntourism' and 'orphanage tourism'. This practice includes travellers coming from abroad to volunteer or visit orphanages or other child care facilities.[217] Considering that the travellers are willing to pay fees for the volunteer experience or orphanage visit, and often consequently donate money or goods, this practice has become a lucrative business.[218] As children are the main commodity soliciting the visits and the donations, orphanages often convince parents and guardians to give children into their care, with the promise of a good education and a 'better future' for the children or simply against payment.[219] As an example, a study has shown that 80–85% of so-called 'orphans' living in orphanages in Nepal and Haiti actually have at least one living parent or close family member.[220] Further, these orphanages are strategically positioned in the main tourist areas to provide easy access to these facilities and promote voluntourism and orphanage tourism.[221]

Depending on the circumstances, these practices can amount to 'sale of children' under the OPSC or 'child trafficking' under the Palermo Protocol.[222] If remuneration or other consideration is given to the child's family in exchange for the child, and the intention is to 'solely' use the child as a 'bait' for orphanage tourism without pursuing any other exploitative purpose as spelled out in the Palermo Protocol, this practice can be considered 'sale of children'. On the other hand, if

---

[214] ECPAT, *Global study on sexual exploitation of children in travel and tourism*, p. 14.

[215] Maalla M'jid, *Report of the Special Rapporteur on the sale of children, child prostitution and child pornography*, A/HRC/22/54, paras. 46 et seq.

[216] ECPAT, *Explanatory Report to the Guidelines Regarding the Implementation of the Optional Protocol to the Convention on the Rights of the Child on the Sale of Children, Child Prostitution and Child Pornography*, p. 49.

[217] Ibid., p. 36.

[218] Maud de Boer-Buquicchio, *Report of the special rapporteur on the sale of children, child prostitution and child pornography*, A/71/261 (1 August 2016), para. 62.

[219] ECPAT, *Global study on sexual exploitation of children in travel and tourism*, p. 40.

[220] US Department of State, *Trafficking in Persons Report 2021*, Washington 2021, pp. 271, 413.

[221] Ibid., p. 413.

[222] For an in-depth examination of the linkages between institutionalization of children and human trafficking, see Lumos, *Cycles of exploitation: the links between children's institutions and human trafficking*, London 2021.

the intended purpose of exploitation falls under the definition of 'child trafficking' in the Palermo Protocol, for example sexual exploitation or forced labour, this practice might be better categorised as 'child trafficking'. Regardless of the exact legal subsummation, these practices are harmful to children and at a minimum, deprive the child of their right to grow up in their family environment as guaranteed under Art 8 CRC.

Further, children in institutionalised care are more vulnerable to abuse, neglect and exploitation. Many volunteers and orphanage tourists are not vetted, yet are put in close, often unsupervised contact with children. Further, voluntourists with a sexual interest in children pay for the privilege of spending time alone with the children.[223] This tremendously increases the risk of sexual abuse and exploitation, including exploitation in prostitution and child sexual abuse material as set out in the OPSC.[224]

This shows that the practice of voluntourism and orphanage tourism causes multi-dimensional harm to children. Children are deprived of growing up in their family environment and possibly subjected to 'sale of children' or 'child trafficking' in the process.

3.2.2.4 'Child Pornography'

3.2.2.4.1 Terminology
Art 2 (c) defines 'child pornography' as 'any representation, by whatever means, of a child engaged in real or simulated explicit sexual activities or any representation of the sexual parts of a child for primarily sexual purposes'. It is important to note that the CRC Committee endorsed a terminology shift away from 'child pornography'.[225] The reasoning is that 'pornography' usually describes adults engaging in consensual sexual activity which is depicted and distributed for sexual arousal. Therefore, the labelling of 'child sexual abuse material' as 'pornography' might create the impression that the child is consenting to the sexual activity and hence it can be categorised as legitimate sexual material.[226] Therefore, the CRC Committee recommends using the terms suggested in the Luxembourg

---

[223] ECPAT, *Global study on sexual exploitation of children in travel and tourism*, p. 58.
[224] Ibid., p. 62.
[225] CRC Committee, *Guidelines regarding the implementation of the Optional Protocol to the Convention on the Rights of the Child on the sale of children, child prostitution and child pornography*, CRC/C/156, para. 60.
[226] For a detailed explanation of these recommended terms see ECPAT, *Terminology Guidelines for the Protection of Children from Sexual Exploitation and Sexual Abuse*, pp. 35 et seq.

Guidelines,[227] which recommend the terms 'use of children in pornographic performances and materials', 'child sexual abuse material' or 'child sexual exploitation material'.[228]

3.2.2.4.2 'Any Representation, by Whatever Means, of a Child'
This phrasing reflects the vast variety of depictions of child sexual abuse material, including, but not limited to, visual, audio, and written material, as well physical objects such as sculptures.[229] The CRC Committee in its Guidelines stresses that both hard and soft copy depictions are covered by this provision.[230] It is hereby not important whether the depiction is firmly materialised and not just temporary: live stream shows are equally covered by the provision, even where there is no recording available.[231]

Heavily debated is the question of what constitutes a 'child' under the OPSC. The OPSC does not define this term, so reference is made to the definition in Art 1 CRC which defines a child as a person below the age of 18 years. However, the question is whether also virtual children as well as persons made to appear as children should fall under this definition.

The CRC Committee encourages States parties to include 'non-existing children or persons appearing to be children' under child sexual abuse material provisions.[232] Firstly, it is important to note that virtual depictions of existing children are covered by the provision ('by whatever means').[233] The issue of non-existing virtual children has been heavily debated across the world, as some courts ruled that there is insufficient scientific proof that the depiction of sexual activity with virtual children leads to either an increase in accessing 'real' child sexual abuse material or

---

[227] CRC Committee, *Guidelines regarding the implementation of the Optional Protocol to the Convention on the Rights of the Child on the sale of children, child prostitution and child pornography*, CRC/C/156, para. 5.

[228] ECPAT, *Terminology Guidelines for the Protection of Children from Sexual Exploitation and Sexual Abuse*, pp. 35 et seq.

[229] Ibid., p. 36.

[230] CRC Committee, *Guidelines regarding the implementation of the Optional Protocol to the Convention on the Rights of the Child on the sale of children, child prostitution and child pornography*, CRC/C/156, para. 61.

[231] ECPAT, *Explanatory Report to the Guidelines Regarding the Implementation of the Optional Protocol to the Convention on the Rights of the Child on the Sale of Children, Child Prostitution and Child Pornography*, p. 66.

[232] CRC Committee, *Guidelines regarding the implementation of the Optional Protocol to the Convention on the Rights of the Child on the sale of children, child prostitution and child pornography*, CRC/C/156, para. 63.

[233] Arguing that even computer-created images can directly harm children if they depict a. the fictional sexual abuse of a real child or b. the actual sexual abuse of a real child, Suzanne Ost, *Criminalising fabricated images of child pornography: a matter of harm or morality?*, Legal Studies, Vol. 30 (2010), p. 232.

contact sexual offences against children. Due to the lack of clear proof of a harmful causality between 'virtual' and 'real' child sexual abuse, the criminalisation of such material would amount to a violation of freedom of speech, which overrules the consideration for potential negative effects on the wellbeing of children.[234]

The main argument against this is that virtual child sexual abuse material contributes to the normalisation of sexualised violence against children and hence has a direct negative effect on children as a group.[235] However, it has to be acknowledged that depictions of a virtual 'child' exist on a scale with life-like, realistic images of fictional children which are hardly identifiable as being virtual on the one end, and the depiction of child-like cartoon characters like fairies on the other end.[236] If the depicted subject has limited resemblance with a 'child' in terms of recognisable human features, one could argue that this is not even a depiction of a 'child' anymore, because the term 'child' might require at least human-like features. It is therefore suggested that the more the material can be qualified as merely 'child-like', yet non-human depictions, artistic end of the scale, the more likely that freedom of expression/artistic freedom aspects prevail.[237]

3.2.2.4.3 'Real or Simulated Explicit Sexual Activities or Any Representation of the Sexual Parts of a Child for Primarily Sexual Purposes'
The definition in Art 2 asks for the criminalisation of 'real or simulated explicit sexual activities'. From the OPSC *travaux préparatoires*, it is clear that the above-mentioned discussion around the inclusion of virtual child sexual abuse material was originally located around the term 'simulated' sexual activities, with Japan advocating for an inclusion of only real children and other countries pushing back on this narrow focus.[238] As the term 'simulated' was retained, the drafting history of the OPSC suggests that virtual child sexual abuse material is clearly covered

---

[234] See for example the reasoning of the US Supreme Court in *Ashcroft v Free Speech Coalition*, 535 US 234 (2002); similar discussions arise in the context of child sex dolls, see Sabine K. Witting, *Child sexual abuse in the digital era—Rethinking legal frameworks and transnational law enforcement collaboration*, Leiden 2020, p. 17; several States parties to the OPSC declared that they understand the term 'any representation' to only cover 'visual representations', for example Belgium, Denmark, Malaysia, Sweden and the United States of America: https://treaties.un.org/pages/ViewDetails .aspx?src=IND&mtdsg_no=IV-11-c&chapter=4 (last accessed: 7 November 2021).

[235] See for example the Canadian Supreme Court in *R v Sharpe* 2001 SCC 2; ECPAT, *Explanatory Report to the Guidelines Regarding the Implementation of the Optional Protocol to the Convention on the Rights of the Child on the Sale of Children, Child Prostitution and Child Pornography*, p. 68.

[236] Witting, *Child sexual abuse in the digital era—Rethinking legal frameworks and transnational law enforcement collaboration*, p. 36.

[237] Ibid.

[238] Tobin, *The Optional Protocol on the Sale of Children, Child Prostitution, and Child Pornography*, p. 1736; however, the formulation of Japan already indicates that the term 'simulated' has nothing to do with the question of whether the child is real or virtual, as the term 'simulated' refers to the sexual activity and not to the child (that is, 'real or simulated explicit sexual activity', rather than a 'real or

under the OPSC. The CRC Committee is more cautious on this subject matter, as it merely 'encourages' States parties to criminalise such material and does not consider it to be part of the legal obligations to criminalise under Arts 2,3.[239] As discussed above, virtual child sexual abuse material is not a homogenous group of materials and hence differentiation needs to be made between punishable realistic images of fictional children which are hardly identifiable as being virtual and merely 'child-like', yet non-human depictions.[240]

The OPSC itself does not offer a further interpretation of the term 'sexual activities'. In the context of 'child prostitution', the CRC Committee offered the following definition of 'sexual activities' which can also be applied here, i.e. 'at a minimum and whether real or simulated, all forms of sexual intercourse and intentional sexual touching involving a child, independent of the sex of all involved persons, and any lascivious exhibition of the genitals or the pubic area of a child'.[241] In the context of 'child pornography', this term is further qualified by the addition of '*explicit* sexual activities'. This means that depictions which merely suggest that children are engaged in sexual activities, such as erotic posing, do not fall under the scope of the OPSC.[242]

The broad definition of the term 'sexual activities' overlaps with the second activity constituting 'child pornography' under the OPSC, the 'representation of the sexual parts of a child for primarily sexual purposes'. According to the *travaux préparatoires*, the sexual parts of a child are not limited to genitalia, but also secondary characteristics such as buttocks and breasts.[243] The CRC Committee acknowledges that for certain imagery, the context in which it is portrayed needs to be considered in order to determine whether it is used for 'primarily sexual purposes'.[244] As an example, the family picture of a naked child in a photo album is not considered to be used for 'primarily sexual purposes', but the same picture

---

simulated child'), see Witting, *Child sexual abuse in the digital era—Rethinking legal frameworks and transnational law enforcement collaboration*, p. 36.

[239] CRC Committee, *Guidelines regarding the implementation of the Optional Protocol to the Convention on the Rights of the Child on the sale of children, child prostitution and child pornography*, CRC/C/156, para. 63.

[240] For a more in-depth discussion on this subject matter, see section 3.2.2.4.

[241] CRC Committee, *Guidelines regarding the implementation of the Optional Protocol to the Convention on the Rights of the Child on the sale of children, child prostitution and child pornography*, CRC/C/156, para. 53.

[242] Tobin, *The Optional Protocol on the Sale of Children, Child Prostitution, and Child Pornography*, p. 1738.

[243] Ibid.

[244] CRC Committee, *Guidelines regarding the implementation of the Optional Protocol to the Convention on the Rights of the Child on the sale of children, child prostitution and child pornography*, CRC/C/156, para. 62.

put on a website for child sexual abuse material might render the same image—due to the context in which it is used—child sexual abuse material.[245] Further, the material needs to be used for *'primarily* sexual purposes'. This means that the material does not need to solely serve sexual purposes, however, where it can be proven that the purposes of the material was only incidentally and not primarily sexual, such material is not considered 'child pornography' under the OPSC.[246]

3.2.2.4.4 Emerging Forms of Online Child Sexual Abuse and Exploitation

Apart from the child sexual abuse material offences covered under Art 2, the CRC Committee in its Guidelines draws attention to other forms of online child sexual abuse and exploitation which require dedicated attention. The National Center for Missing and Exploited Children noted a 97.5 % increase in 'online enticement' cases in 2020, which includes grooming.[247] The CRC Committee defines 'grooming' as a 'process of establishing a relationship with a child either in person or through the use of ICT to facilitate online or offline sexual contact'.[248] In order to avoid detection, perpetrators move the conversation from public to private messaging platforms or use multiple platforms at the same time.[249] Grooming is not explicitly mentioned in the OPSC, however, the CRC Committee stresses that grooming can occur in the context of Art 2 and hence fall under the scope of the OPSC.[250] It is noteworthy that other international instruments have gone a step further and explicitly criminalised grooming, such as Art 23 Lanzarote Convention ('Solicitation of children for sexual purposes'). However, the process of intentionally contacting a child online alone to facilitate sexual contact is not sufficient for conduct to be considered illegal. The proposal to meet offline must be followed by material acts leading to such a meeting.[251] This definition requires updating to also include situations whereby the abuse is perpetrated solely online.[252]

---

[245] ECPAT, *Explanatory Report to the Guidelines Regarding the Implementation of the Optional Protocol to the Convention on the Rights of the Child on the Sale of Children, Child Prostitution and Child Pornography*, p. 67.

[246] Tobin, *The Optional Protocol on the Sale of Children, Child Prostitution, and Child Pornography*, p. 1739.

[247] WeProtect Global Alliance, *Global Threat Assessment 2021*, p. 36.

[248] CRC Committee, *Guidelines regarding the implementation of the Optional Protocol to the Convention on the Rights of the Child on the sale of children, child prostitution and child pornography*, CRC/C/156, para. 68.

[249] WeProtect Global Alliance, *Global Threat Assessment 2021*, p. 37.

[250] CRC Committee, *Guidelines regarding the implementation of the Optional Protocol to the Convention on the Rights of the Child on the sale of children, child prostitution and child pornography*, CRC/C/156, para. 68.

[251] See Art 23 Lanzarote Convention.

[252] WeProtect Global Alliance, *Global Threat Assessment 2021*, p. 36.

The CRC Committee defines 'sexual extortion' as 'a practice whereby a child is forced into agreeing to give sexual favours, money or other benefits under the threat of sexual material depicting the child being shared on, for example, social media'.[253] Sexual extortion is often linked to grooming or 'sexting' (see section 3.2.2.4.5 for more details), whereby the initial material which is later used to black-mail the child might have been shared voluntarily by the child as part of an initial exchange between child and perpetrator.[254] Another strategy is to juxtapose images of victims on pornographic images from other sources, and then threaten the child to widely disseminate this material or directly send it to the child's family and friends.[255] Other contemporary forms of online child sexual abuse are made-to-order services and live-streaming. Made-to-order services allow the perpetrator to request the production of content in which the age, gender and race of the child are specified according to the perpetrator's sexual preferences.[256] Livestreaming of online child sexual abuse is another emerging form in which perpetrators can buy access to the live stream to observe the abuse in real time.[257] This can involve the livestreaming of sexual abuse of a child, or a child who is forced to perform sexual acts in front of a webcam.[258] In contrast to other forms of child sexual abuse and exploitation, livestreaming seems to be primarily financially motivated. In the Philippines, most persons involved in livestreaming were financially motivated female relatives or close associates of the victim. Livestreaming facilitated by family members is often justified by stating that children need to contribute to their family's income and the wrong belief that due to the lack of physical interaction with the clients, livestreaming is not harmful to children.[259] In the context of livestreaming, 'capping' has been identified as an increasing trend, whereby perpetrators produce additional material of children during livestreams by capturing them on their camera and sharing it further.[260]

The CRC Committee stresses that especially in the context of ICT-facilitated child abuse and exploitation, it is crucial to consider technological advancements and regularly assess the efficacy of the legal framework to combat emerging trends. If

---

[253] CRC Committee, *Guidelines regarding the implementation of the Optional Protocol to the Convention on the Rights of the Child on the sale of children, child prostitution and child pornography*, para. 69.
[254] Ibid.
[255] UNODC, *Study on the Effects of New Information Technologies on the Abuse of Children*, p. 12.
[256] Ibid., p. 21.
[257] Ibid., pp. 22–23.
[258] WeProtect Global Alliance, *Global Threat Assessment 2021*, p. 60.
[259] Ibid., p. 63.
[260] For a definition and closer analysis of this phenomenon, see ibid., pp. 42, 70.

necessary, laws and policies should be swiftly amended to adequately respond to rapidly changing realities.[261]

3.2.2.4.5 Non-exploitative 'Child Pornography'?—The Case of Consensual 'Sexting' between Children

Child 'self-generated' sexual material comprises an increasing proportion of child sexual abuse material available online. The Internet Watch Foundation has registered a 77% increase in 'self-generated' child sexual abuse material between 2019 and 2020 and notes that around 44% of all imagery analysed by them is considered 'self-generated'. Importantly, the category of 'self-generated' material includes both voluntary produced and coerced material. According to the CRC Committee, any material which is 'self-generated' as a result of coercion or blackmail, is categorised as child sexual abuse material.[262] However, considering that voluntary material is often shared between adolescents as part of a developmentally appropriate exchange, the legal and policy response needs to take these different dynamics into consideration.[263]

The discussion around the appropriate legal and policy response to 'self-generated' material is particularly complex in the context of the OPSC as it reflects on one of the major contradictions between the CRC and the OPSC. The CRC only prohibits the 'exploitative' use of children for pornographic material, whereas the OPSC prohibits any form of pornographic material depicting children, regardless of whether it is considered exploitative or not.

This differentiation plays an important role when it comes to the production and sharing of voluntary 'self-generated' material, also called 'sexting'.[264] Online sexual exploration such as 'sexting' is becoming a significant component of teenagers' sexuality.[265] Sexuality, identity, intimacy, and interpersonal connection are matters of interest to teenagers in their journey of identity exploration and construction. While these areas have been traditionally explored and constructed in

---

[261] CRC Committee, *Guidelines regarding the implementation of the Optional Protocol to the Convention on the Rights of the Child on the sale of children, child prostitution and child pornography*, CRC/C/156, para. 19.

[262] CRC Committee, *Guidelines regarding the implementation of the Optional Protocol to the Convention on the Rights of the Child on the sale of children, child prostitution and child pornography*, CRC/C/156, para. 67.

[263] WeProtect Global Alliance, *Global Threat Assessment 2021*, p. 54.

[264] The term is a portmanteau of the words 'sex' and 'texting' and describes self-produced sexually suggestive or explicit images and texts that are distributed by cell phone messaging, Internet messenger, social networks and the like, see UNICEF, *Regulation of Child Online Sexual Abuse. Legal Analysis of International Law & Comparative Legal Analysis*, Windhoek 2016, p. 16.

[265] Noting that teenagers increasingly consider sexting to be 'normal', CRC Committee, *Guidelines regarding the implementation of the Optional Protocol to the Convention on the Rights of the Child on the sale of children, child prostitution and child pornography*, CRC/C/156, para. 42.

offline interactions between the self and others, an increasingly important realm for such activities is the Internet.[266] With teenage 'sexting' material and 'child pornography' as defined in the OPSC objectively depicting the same behaviour, i.e. sexual activity involving a child, the law in many countries does not differentiate between the circumstances under which the material was produced but criminalises the production, dissemination and possession of both groups of materials as 'child pornography' offences.[267]

The CRC Committee in its guidelines acknowledges that 'sexting' is increasingly considered normal by adolescents.[268] It rightfully stresses that there are numerous risks associated with this practice, as the material might be further shared with third parties against the will of the child or be used in the context of bullying.[269] Considering these risks, some have argued in favour of a criminalisation of teenage 'sexting' either as 'child pornography' offence or as separate, more lenient criminal offence. The arguments for such criminalisation focus on the risks related to teenage sexting and the deterrent effect of such legislation.[270] Children, and in particular girls, are hence deprived of any sexuality, let alone a right to express such sexuality, and seem to be granted only a right to protection from sexual exploitation.[271] This stands in stark contrast to the rights under Art 16 CRC discussed in section 2.1.1. Instead of solely focusing on the right to protection, a balanced approach between Arts 16, 19 and 34 CRC is required. Such a balanced approach was established for the first time in an international treaty through Art 20 (3) Lanzarote Convention. It states that material depicting children who

---

[266] Smahel/ Subrahmanyam, *Adolescent Sexuality on the Internet: A Developmental Perspective*, p. 62.

[267] Witting, *Child sexual abuse in the digital era—Rethinking legal frameworks and transnational law enforcement collaboration*, p. 41.

[268] CRC Committee, *Guidelines regarding the implementation of the Optional Protocol to the Convention on the Rights of the Child on the sale of children, child prostitution and child pornography*, CRC/C/156, para. 42.

[269] Ibid.

[270] For a comprehensive overview of the debate around sexting and its potential harm for children, see Witting, *Child sexual abuse in the digital era—Rethinking legal frameworks and transnational law enforcement collaboration*, p. 39; Alisdair A. Gillespie, *Adolescents, Sexting and Human Rights*, Human Rights Law Review, Vol. 13 (2013), pp. 626 et seq.; see further the arguments put forward in Megan Sherman, *Sixteen, Sexting, and a Sex Offender: How Advances in Cell Phone Technology Have Led to Teenage Sex Offenders*, Boston University Journal for Science and Technology Law, Vol. 17 (2011), pp. 157–158; Mary Graw Leary, *Self-Produced Child Pornography: The Appropriate Societal Response to Juvenile Self-Sexual Exploitation*, Virginia Journal of Social Policy and Law, Vol. 15 (2008), p. 39.

[271] Witting, *Child sexual abuse in the digital era—Rethinking legal frameworks and transnational law enforcement collaboration*, p. 62; Belinda Carpenter et al., *Harm, Responsibility, Age, and Consent*, New Criminal Law Review: An International and Interdisciplinary Journal, Vol. 17 (2014), p. 31; arguing that adults have been preventing children from understanding and experiencing their own sexuality by tabooing child sexuality, Kate Millet, *Beyond Politics? Children and Sexuality* in: Carole S. Vance (ed.), *Pleasure and Danger. Exploring female sexuality*, Boston 1984, pp. 218–219.

have reached the age of consent to sexual activity and where these images are produced and possessed by them with their consent and solely for their own private use, States parties can exempt such content from the range of the 'child pornography' definition.[272] The CRC Committee in its Guidelines follows this practice and makes it clear that 'States parties should not criminalize adolescents of similar ages for consensual sexual activity'[273] and applies the same standard to online sexual activity, stating that 'children should not be held criminally liable for producing images of themselves'.[274] At the same time, the Committee also recognises that in cases where initially consensually produced material is further distributed without the consent of the depicted child, the distributors should be held criminally liable.[275]

This response to the complex issue of consensual 'sexting' between children shows that the CRC Committee through the Guidelines rejects the welfarist approach postulated in the OPSC and consequently reinvokes the conceptualisation of Art 34 CRC by recognising that not all 'child pornography' is automatically exploitative.

3.2.3 *Art 3 OPSC: Obligation to Criminalise*

3.2.3.1 Art 3 (1): Sale of Children, 'Child Prostitution' and 'Child Pornography'

Article 3
1. Each State Party shall ensure that, as a minimum, the following acts and activities are fully covered under its criminal or penal law, whether such offences are committed domestically or transnationally or on an individual or organized basis:

---

[272] For an in-depth discussion around exemption clauses from an international, regional, and national perspective, see Witting, *Child sexual abuse in the digital era—Rethinking legal frameworks and transnational law enforcement collaboration*, pp. 36 et seq.

[273] See also CRC Committee, *Guidelines regarding the implementation of the Optional Protocol to the Convention on the Rights of the Child on the sale of children, child prostitution and child pornography*, CRC/C/156, para. 73; acknowledging that the setting of an age of sexual consent recognises children's evolving capacities, ECPAT, *Explanatory Report to the Guidelines Regarding the Implementation of the Optional Protocol to the Convention on the Rights of the Child on the Sale of Children, Child Prostitution and Child Pornography*, p. 74.

[274] CRC Committee, *Guidelines regarding the implementation of the Optional Protocol to the Convention on the Rights of the Child on the sale of children, child prostitution and child pornography*, CRC/C/156, para. 67; CRC Committee, *General comment No. 25 (2021) on children's rights in relation to the digital environment*, CRC/C/GC/25, para. 118; see also the declaration from Denmark on the OPSC, stating that 'the possession of pornographic visual representation of a person, who has completed their fifteenth year and who has consented to said possession, shall not be considered covered by the binding provisions of the Protocol', available here: https://treaties.un.org/pages/ViewDetails .aspx?src=IND&mtdsg_no=IV-11-c&chapter=4 (last accessed: 7 November 2021).

[275] CRC Committee, *Guidelines regarding the implementation of the Optional Protocol to the Convention on the Rights of the Child on the sale of children, child prostitution and child pornography*, CRC/C/156, para. 67.

(a) In the context of sale of children as defined in article 2:
   (i) Offering, delivering or accepting, by whatever means, a child for the purpose of:
      a. Sexual exploitation of the child;
      b. Transfer of organs of the child for profit;
      c. Engagement of the child in forced labour;
   (ii) Improperly inducing consent, as an intermediary, for the adoption of a child in violation of applicable international legal instruments on adoption;
(b) Offering, obtaining, procuring or providing a child for child prostitution, as defined in article 2;
(c) Producing, distributing, disseminating, importing, exporting, offering, selling or possessing for the above purposes child pornography as defined in article 2.

3.2.3.1.1 Conceptualisation

Art 3 (1) stipulates the legal obligation of States parties to criminalise all acts contained in this article. The provision needs to be understood as a minimum standard which States parties cannot fall short of. However, they are of course free to enact more far-reaching legislation to protect children. The CRC Committee in its guidelines encourages States parties to introduce new provisions in their criminal or penal law to ensure that they can also adequately address sexual offences against children when newly emerging means and modalities are used to commit them.[276]

Art 3 (1) further states that the obligation to criminalise extends to offences committed both domestically and transnationally, and whether committed by an individual or on an organized basis. This ensures that the broad variety of criminal activity in the context of the OPSC is covered by the obligation to criminalise under Art 3 (1).

3.2.3.1.2 Sale of Children

Art 3 (1) (a) requires States parties to criminalise two forms of sale of children, the first one pertaining to various forms of exploitation and the second targeting illegal adoptions. The first form covers the 'offering, delivering or accepting by whatever means a child for the purpose of sexual exploitation; transfer of organs for profit or engagement of the child in forced labour'. It is important to note here that even though Art 3 (1) connects the sale of children to various forms of exploitation, States parties can exceed this standard and enact legislation which does not require the presence of (intended) exploitation, in line with Art 2. Neither the OPSC nor the OPSC Guidelines offer a definition of the term 'sexual exploitation',

---

[276] CRC Committee, *Guidelines regarding the implementation of the Optional Protocol to the Convention on the Rights of the Child on the sale of children, child prostitution and child pornography,* CRC/C/156, para. 44.

however, as discussed in the context of Art 34 CRC in section 2.1.4, the definition usually includes sexual activity in exchange for something.[277]

The sale of children for the transfer of organs for profit is one of the least discovered areas in the OPSC. However, research and practical guides developed in the context of the Palermo Protocol can be leveraged for a broader understanding of this form of sale of children. Art 3 of the Palermo Protocol criminalises the trafficking in children for the purposes of removal of organs.[278] The choice of the word 'for profit' instead of 'for remuneration or any other form of consideration', which is used in the definitions of sale of children and 'child prostitution' in Art 2, suggest a greater focus based on a financial benefit.[279]

Lastly, the sale of children for the purpose of forced labour needs to be read closely with the relevant ILO Conventions No. 29 (Convention of Forced Labour), No. 105 (Convention in the Abolition of Forced Labour) and No. 182 (Convention on the Worst Forms of Child Labour). ILO Convention No. 29 defines forced labour as 'all work or service which is extracted from any person under the menace of any penalty and for which the said person had not offered himself voluntarily'. Children are sold and engaged in forced labour in a variety of contexts, including domestic work, manufacturing and begging.[280] It is estimated that the agricultural sector employs the largest number of child workers (nearly 60%).[281] Forced child labour can also occur in the context of child marriages, whereby children are forced into domestic and manual labour (see also section 3.2.2).[282]

Art 3 (1) (a) (ii) OPSC criminalises 'the act of improperly inducing consent, as an intermediary, for the adoption of a child in violation of applicable international legal instruments on adoption'. The CRC Committee defines the term 'improperly inducing consent for adoption' as 'obtaining consent for the adoption of a child in a dishonest or inappropriate manner', which includes *inter alia* the use of remunerations or other considerations.[283] This provision only targets intermediaries

---

[277] See also Tobin, *The Optional Protocol on the Sale of Children, Child Prostitution, and Child Pornography*, p. 1742.

[278] See for example UNODC, *Assessment Toolkit—Trafficking in Persons for the Purpose of Organ Removal*, Vienna 2015.

[279] Tobin, *The Optional Protocol on the Sale of Children, Child Prostitution, and Child Pornography*, p. 1742.

[280] For an in-depth analysis of the various forms of sale of children for the purpose of forced labour, see de Boer-Buquicchio, *Report of the Special Rapporteur on the sale of children, child prostitution and child pornography*, A/71/261, paras. 29 et seq.

[281] Ibid., para. 34.

[282] ECPAT, *Thematic Report: Unrecognized Sexual Abuse and Exploitation of Children in Child, Early and Forced Marriages*, Bangkok 2015, p. 58.

[283] CRC Committee, *Guidelines regarding the implementation of the Optional Protocol to the Convention on the Rights of the Child on the sale of children, child prostitution and child pornography*, CRC/C/156, para. 50.

such as private adoption agencies, whose business model is based on facilitating intercountry adoptions with the payment of fees dependent on the success of the adoption process. This creates an environment where these intermediaries might be tempted to employ dishonest methods to accelerate and facilitate the adoption for their own financial gain, leaving child protection considerations out of the equation.[284] However, it is not clear from the drafting history why the OPSC has such a narrow focus when it comes to the sale of children in relation to intercountry adoptions.[285] There are plenty of other criminal acts committed in the intercountry adoption process, such as the kidnapping of children for the purpose of adoption, which have a devastating impact on the rights of these children[286] but are not covered by the OPSC as consent was plainly not present (and hence not induced). Considering that Art 3 (1) only sets out a minimum standard, States parties are encouraged to criminalise other harmful acts in the context of intercountry adoptions.[287] Further, the adoption must violate 'applicable international legal instruments on adoption'. The CRC Committee in its Guidelines clarified that this covers Art 21 CRC as well as the Hague Convention on Protection of Children and Cooperation in respect of Intercountry Adoption (1993).[288] In this context, the question arises whether these international instruments also apply via the OPSC to States parties which have not ratified them. The CRC Committee has not addressed this question directly.[289] However, considering the clear language of the OPSC Guidelines, and the fact that States parties ratifying the OPSC were at least aware of the 'risk' to be also bound by international adoption conventions, it can be assumed that the content of these provisions is indeed integrated into the relevant provisions of the OPSC. This interpretation is further confirmed by several states making explicit declarations not to be bound by any international treaties on intercountry adoption by the mere fact of being a State party to the OPSC.[290]

---

[284] Maud de Boer-Buquicchio, *Report of the Special Rapporteur on the sale of children, child prostitution and child pornography*, A/HRC/34/55 (22 December 2016), paras. 65–66.

[285] Tobin, *The Optional Protocol on the Sale of Children, Child Prostitution, and Child Pornography*, p. 1744.

[286] de Boer-Buquicchio, *Report of the Special Rapporteur on the sale of children, child prostitution and child pornography*, A/HRC/34/55, para. 28.

[287] Tobin, *The Optional Protocol on the Sale of Children, Child Prostitution, and Child Pornography*, p. 1744.

[288] CRC Committee, *Guidelines regarding the implementation of the Optional Protocol to the Convention on the Rights of the Child on the sale of children, child prostitution and child pornography*, CRC/C/156, para. 50.

[289] Tobin, *The Optional Protocol on the Sale of Children, Child Prostitution, and Child Pornography*, p. 1744.

[290] See declarations from Argentina, Malaysia, Korea and the United States of America, and the reservation entered by Syria here: https://treaties.un.org/pages/ViewDetails.aspx?src=IND&mtdsg_no=IV-11-c&chapter=4 (last accessed: 7 November 2021).

3.2.3.1.3 'Child Prostitution'
Art 3 (1) (b) requires States parties to criminalise the 'offering, obtaining, procuring or providing a child for child prostitution, as defined in Art 2'. The terminology used in this provision suggests that it targets intermediaries who facilitate
the exploitation of a child in prostitution. However, the ordinary meaning of the
terms could also indicate that a child who offers him- or herself for prostitution
could be covered by the provision and hence be prosecuted. The CRC Committee
in its Guidelines made it clear that States parties must ensure that 'national legislation does not criminalise children exploited in acts that would constitute an
offence under the Optional Protocol but treat them as victims'.[291]

3.2.3.1.4 'Child Pornography'
Art 3 (1) (c) requires States parties to criminalise the acts of 'producing, distributing, disseminating, importing, exporting, offering, selling or possessing for the
above purposes child pornography as defined in Article 2'. Whether the mere possession of 'child pornography' is covered by Art 3(1)(c), has been vividly debated
since the enactment of the OPSC. The main question is whether 'for the above
purposes' refers to 'producing, distributing, disseminating, importing, exporting,
offering, selling', or—as per the suggestion in the CRC Committee's Guidelines—
to 'sexual exploitation'.[292] The latter proposal clearly changes the language of
the provision, as there is no mentioning of possession for the 'purpose of sexual
exploitation'. The CRC Committee seems to correct itself already in the next sentence by 'strongly encouraging' States parties to extend their criminal provisions
to the 'mere possession' of such material,[293] thereby suggesting that 'mere possession' is not covered by the current wording of the OPSC.

Another gap in the OPSC considers the 'accessing' of child sexual abuse material. In such a case, the material is only streamed and not downloaded, hence not
possessed, and therefore clearly falls outside the scope of the OPSC. Emerging
trends in which this differentiation becomes relevant is the livestreaming of child

---

[291] CRC Committee, *Guidelines regarding the implementation of the Optional Protocol to the
Convention on the Rights of the Child on the sale of children, child prostitution and child pornography*,
CRC/C/156, para. 18.
[292] CRC Committee, *Guidelines regarding the implementation of the Optional Protocol to the
Convention on the Rights of the Child on the sale of children, child prostitution and child pornography*,
CRC/C/156, para. 65; advocating for an interpretation of art 3(1)(c) which allows lawful exceptions
to the possession of child sexual abuse material, e.g. for law enforcement and medical profession-
als, ECPAT, *Explanatory Report to the Guidelines Regarding the Implementation of the Optional
Protocol to the Convention on the Rights of the Child on the Sale of Children, Child Prostitution and
Child Pornography*, p. 69.
[293] CRC Committee, *Guidelines regarding the implementation of the Optional Protocol to the
Convention on the Rights of the Child on the sale of children, child prostitution and child pornography*,
CRC/C/156, para. 65.

sexual abuse (see section 3.2.2.4). While the CRC Committee acknowledges live streaming as an emerging threat[294] and calls for States parties to introduce criminal provisions which cover 'newly emerging means and modalities,'[295] it missed the opportunity in the Guidelines to explicitly request States parties to include the accessing of child sexual abuse material in their criminal provisions. It should hereby have followed the wording of Art 20 (1) Lanzarote Convention, which explicitly criminalises 'knowingly obtaining access [...] to child pornography'.

3.2.3.2 Art 3 (2): Attempt, Complicity and Participation

> 2. Subject to the provisions of the national law of a State Party, the same shall apply to an attempt to commit any of the said acts and to complicity or participation in any of the said acts.

The OPSC stipulates that States parties are obliged to criminalise attempt to commit any OPSC offences as well as complicity and participation in any such offences.[296] Instead of coming up with a universal definition of these terms, the CRC Committee leaves it to the States parties to concretise attempt, participation and complicity.[297] The obligation hence only extends to the *if* of the regulation, not the *how*. This makes sense, as the definition of these terms is an inherent part of each country's national criminal law system and prescribing certain definitions and concepts would have affected the entire criminal law system even beyond the offences contained in the OPSC.

While acknowledging the States parties' sovereignty to regulate these terms on national level, the explanatory report to the Guidelines gives guidance on the meaning of these terms. For attempt, it states that this should include the intent to commit the act, a substantive step towards completing the relevant act and the failure to complete the act. In the context of the OPSC, it states that contacting a child for the purpose of sexually abusing or exploiting them should be considered an attempt to commit a criminal offence. Complicity is often referred to as 'aiding and abetting' and is particularly relevant in the context of the OPSC for people who provide the means for the commission of a crime, for example

---

[294] CRC Committee, *Guidelines regarding the implementation of the Optional Protocol to the Convention on the Rights of the Child on the sale of children, child prostitution and child pornography*, CRC/C/156, paras. 2, 87.

[295] Ibid., para. 44.

[296] Ibid., paras. 45, 78.

[297] Tobin, *The Optional Protocol on the Sale of Children, Child Prostitution, and Child Pornography*, p. 1748.

by providing premises or technological means which facilitate sexual offences against children.[298]

3.2.3.3   Art 3 (3): Penalties

> 3. Each State Party shall make such offences punishable by appropriate penalties that take into account their grave nature.

States Parties are obliged to enact criminal laws with 'appropriate' penalties. Even though the exact range of sentence is prescribed on national level, States parties must take the 'grave nature' of the offences under the OPSC into account.[299]

A prominent discussion in this context is the issue of mandatory minimum sentences. Mandatory minimum sentences stipulate a minimum threshold for a specific category of criminal offences and aim to ensure that certain crimes are not dealt with in a 'lenient' manner. Mandatory minimum sentences considerably limit the court's ability to take the specific circumstances of each individual case into account[300] in lieu of a more consistent sentencing regime across the same category of offences. However, some countries encountered constitutional challenges with minimum mandatory sentences due to the risk of imposing disproportionate sentences. To mitigate the risk of declaring statutory minimum sentencing regimes unconstitutional, deviating from the minimum sentence is permissible in 'substantial and compelling circumstances'. The problem with this 'backdoor' is that there is a considerable risk that the exception becomes the rule, *de facto* undermining the minimum sentencing regime.[301] Other countries only allow an exception from the mandatory minimums if the defendant provides 'substantial assistance' to law enforcement.[302] Regardless of the approach States parties take to the issue of mandatory minimums, it is important that the imposition of harsher sentences is not a scapegoat for addressing the root causes of offences

---

[298] ECPAT, *Explanatory Report to the Guidelines Regarding the Implementation of the Optional Protocol to the Convention on the Rights of the Child on the Sale of Children, Child Prostitution and Child Pornography*, p. 55.

[299] CRC Committee, *Guidelines regarding the implementation of the Optional Protocol to the Convention on the Rights of the Child on the sale of children, child prostitution and child pornography*, CRC/C/156, para. 77.

[300] ECPAT, *Explanatory Report to the Guidelines Regarding the Implementation of the Optional Protocol to the Convention on the Rights of the Child on the Sale of Children, Child Prostitution and Child Pornography*, p. 78.

[301] Discussing the benefits and disadvantages of the mandatory minimum sentencing regime in South Africa, see Kristina Scurry Baehr, *Mandatory Minimums Making Minimal Difference: Ten Years of Sentencing Sex Offenders in South Africa*, Yale Journal of Law and Feminism, Vol. 20 (1), pp. 213 et seq.

[302] United States Sentencing Commission, *Mandatory Minimum Penalties for Sex Offences in the Federal Criminal Justice System*, Washington 2019, p. 11.

under the OPSC. Sentencing regimes are commonly politicised to distract from the failure of the current prevention and response strategies. As increasing the sentences is usually a fairly quick process which may trigger positive responses from the general public, it is crucial to note that sentencing regimes are just one amongst many interventions to prevent the OPSC offences, which will be discussed in more detail in section 3.2.9.

In the same vein, States parties must consider the appropriateness of sentences if the offender is a child. Considering the common misconception that all juvenile sex offenders turn into adult sex offenders, it is key that states respond to juvenile offenders in line with the principles set out in the CRC and other relevant instruments for children in conflict with the law.[303]

In addition, the child victim's voice is crucial to determine the appropriateness of the sentence in each individual case. Therefore, States parties need to ensure that the affected child gets the opportunity to participate in the sentencing process, for example through victim impact statements. This will be discussed in more detail in section 3.2.8.1.

3.2.3.4 Art 3 (4): Liability of Legal Persons

4. Subject to the provisions of its national law, each State Party shall take measures, where appropriate, to establish the liability of legal persons for offences established in paragraph 1 of the present article. Subject to the legal principles of the State Party, such liability of legal persons may be criminal, civil or administrative.

Art 3 (4) sets out the role of the business sector in relation to the offences under the OPSC. While businesses play a critical role in enhancing children's rights, in particular in this globalised and digitalised world,[304] individuals engaging in OPSC offences often leverage institutional and business structures which enable and aid child violations to take place.[305] In line with the UN Guiding Principles on Business and Human Rights,[306] the CRC Committee conceptualises this

---

[303] CRC Committee, *Guidelines regarding the implementation of the Optional Protocol to the Convention on the Rights of the Child on the sale of children, child prostitution and child pornography*, CRC/C/156, para. 71; ECPAT, *Explanatory Report to the Guidelines Regarding the Implementation of the Optional Protocol to the Convention on the Rights of the Child on the Sale of Children, Child Prostitution and Child Pornography*, p. 78.

[304] CRC Committee, *General comment No. 16 (2013) on State obligations regarding the impact of the business sector on children's rights*, CRC/C/GC/16, para. 1.

[305] Tobin, *The Optional Protocol on the Sale of Children, Child Prostitution, and Child Pornography*, p. 1749.

[306] UN, *Guiding Principles on Business and Human Rights*, New York 2011.

responsibility to encompass both a legal responsibility in case of child rights violations as well as a responsibility to prevent and mitigate them.[307]

Regarding the responsibility of legal persons, it is important to note that this is a mandatory obligation for States parties ('shall'). The qualification 'subject to the provisions of its national law' should not be misunderstood to enable States parties to render this obligation meaningless: it merely gives States parties the discretion to regulate the 'how', but not the 'if' of the responsibility of legal persons for OPSC violations.[308] In principle, States parties are free to decide whether they impose criminal, civil and/or administrative sanctions on legal persons. However, the CRC Committee recommends criminal liability or any other form of legal liability with the same deterrent effect for legal persons involved in child rights violations.[309] The CRC Committee in its Concluding Observations for Russia and Saudi Arabia highlighted that these States should include a criminal liability for legal persons engaged in any offences under the OPSC.[310]

The CRC Committee further highlights the responsibility of specific sectors relevant for the offences under the OPSC, asking States parties to 'establish by the law the responsibility of ICT companies to block and remove child sexual abuse material hosted on their servers, of financial institutions to block and refuse financial transaction intended to pay for any such offences, of the sport and entertainment industries to take child protective measures, and of the travel and tourism sector, including travel agencies and booking websites, to refrain from facilitating the sexual exploitation of children'.[311] Any measure undertaken by the private sector should be informed by evidence. A child-rights impact assessment is a crucial first step to identify the business' impact on children's rights and should lead

---

[307] CRC Committee, *Guidelines regarding the implementation of the Optional Protocol to the Convention on the Rights of the Child on the sale of children, child prostitution and child pornography*, para. 79.

[308] Tobin, *The Optional Protocol on the Sale of Children, Child Prostitution, and Child Pornography*, p. 1750.

[309] CRC Committee, *General comment No. 16 (2013) on State obligations regarding the impact of the business sector on children's rights*, CRC/C/GC/16 (17 April 2013), para. 70.

[310] CRC Committee, *Concluding observations on the report submitted by the Russian Federation under article 12 (1) of the Optional Protocol to the Convention on the Rights of the Child on the sale of children, child prostitution and child pornography*, CRC/C/OPSC/RUS/CO/01, paras. 30, 31; CRC Committee, *Concluding observations on the report submitted by Saudi Arabia under article 12 (1) of the Optional Protocol to the Convention on the Rights of the Child on the sale of children, child prostitution and child pornography*, CRC/C/OPSC/SAU/CO/1, paras. 30, 31.

[311] CRC Committee, *Guidelines regarding the implementation of the Optional Protocol to the Convention on the Rights of the Child on the sale of children, child prostitution and child pornography*, CRC/C/156, para. 79.

to the development of clear recommendations for improvements.[312] A concrete example for mitigative measures in the context of child online safety is the development of age-appropriate information on how to manage online risks and where to seek help.[313] Best practices to combat child sexual abuse and exploitation in travel and tourism include training of staff to identify and respond to risks of child rights violations or to play educative videos about SECTT during flights to high-risk destinations.[314]

In summary, holding legal persons responsible for committing, enabling or facilitating OPSC offences is a key instrument to hold the private sector accountable. Moreover, concrete action is required from industry to take active steps in preventing and mitigating the risk of OPSC violations from happening in the first place.

3.2.3.5 Art 3 (5): Measures regarding Intercountry Adoption

> 5. States Parties shall take all appropriate legal and administrative measures to ensure that all persons involved in the adoption of a child act in conformity with applicable international legal instruments.

This provision is closely linked to the provisions on protection of children from unlawful international adoptions set out in Art 21 CRC and Art 3 (1) (a) (ii). It is broader than the obligation to criminalise certain forms of intercountry adoption in the context of sale of children and asks States parties to take all appropriate measures to ensure applicable international legal instruments are complied with. Even though this provision does not add any additional value for states who have ratified the CRC and relevant international treaties on intercountry adoption, it incorporates those legal instruments into the OPSC and hence also makes

---

[312] CRC Committee, *General comment No. 16 (2013) on State obligations regarding the impact of the business sector on children's rights*, CRC/C/GC/16, para. 79; CRC Committee, *General comment No. 25 (2021) on children's rights in relation to the digital environment*, CRC/C/GC/25, para. 38; UNICEF developed a child rights impact self-assessment tool specifically for mobile operators, see here: https://www.unicef.org/reports/mo-cria-child-rights-impact-self-assessment-tool-mobile-operators (last accessed: 7 November 2021).

[313] CRC Committee, *General comment No. 16 (2013) on State obligations regarding the impact of the business sector on children's rights*, CRC/C/GC/16, para. 60; for more information on the roles and responsibilities of industry in the context of child online safety, see ITU, *Guidelines on Child Online Protection*, Geneva 2020, available here: https://www.itu-cop-guidelines.com (last accessed: 7 November 2021); for an evaluation framework measuring the impact of online awareness raising campaigns, see UNICEF East Asia and the Pacific and Young and Resilient Research Centre, *Evaluating Online Safety Initiatives: Building the evidence base on what works to keep children safe online*, Bangkok, 2022.

[314] ECPAT, *Global study on sexual exploitation of children in travel and tourism*, pp. 98–99.

them binding for OPSC States parties which have not explicitly ratified these instruments.[315]

3.2.4 *Art 4 OPSC: Jurisdiction*

The concept of jurisdiction is the corner stone of the justice response to any offences under the OPSC. To understand jurisdiction, it is crucial to grasp its interlinkages with the principle of state sovereignty, which is protected under customary international law.[316] The principle of sovereignty entails that states shall not 'interfere in any form or for any reason whatsoever in the internal and external affairs of other States'.[317] This principle is expressed in three forms of jurisdiction, i.e. jurisdiction to prescribe, jurisdiction to adjudicate and jurisdiction to enforce.[318] Of particular relevance is the jurisdiction to adjudicate, as Art 4 regulates when a state can take legal action against an individual or group of people. In contrast to that, the jurisdiction to enforce entails a state's power to enforce its laws through means of executive or administrative acts.[319]

Jurisdiction is generally based on two principles: territoriality and extra-territoriality.[320] As extra-territorial jurisdiction potentially violates the sovereignty of another state, the default rule is that extra-territorial jurisdiction can only be exercised if there is a specific permissive rule.[321]

3.2.4.1 Art 4 (1) OPSC: Territorial Jurisdiction

> 1. Each State Party shall take such measures as may be necessary to establish its jurisdiction over the offences referred to in Article 3, paragraph 1, when the offences are committed in its territory or on board a ship or aircraft registered in that State.

Article 4 (1) of the OPSC establishes jurisdiction over offences committed on a State party's territory (territorial jurisdiction), including ships and aircrafts

---

[315] Tobin, *The Optional Protocol on the Sale of Children, Child Prostitution, and Child Pornography*, p. 1751.
[316] UNODC, *Comprehensive Study on Cybercrime Draft—February 2013*, New York 2013, p. 184.
[317] See Art 1 of the UN General Assembly, *Declaration on the Inadmissibility of Intervention in the Domestic Affairs of States*, A/RES/36/103 (9 December 1981).
[318] Cedric Ryngaert, *Research Handbook on Jurisdiction and Immunities in International Law*, Cheltenham 2015, pp. 15–17.
[319] Dan Svantesson/Felicity Gerry, *Access to extraterritorial evidence: The Microsoft cloud case and beyond*, Computer Law and Security Review, Vol. 31 (2015), p. 480; Susan W. Brenner/Bert-Jaap Koops, *Approaches to Cybercrime Jurisdiction*, Journal of High Technology Law, Vol. 4 (2004), pp. 5–6; Anna-Maria Osula, *Transborder access and territorial sovereignty*, Computer Law and Security Review, Vol. 31 (2015), p. 721.
[320] Alisdair Gillespie, *Cybercrime. Key Issues and Debates*, Oxon 2019, p. 290.
[321] Stephan Kolossa, *The charm of jurisdictions: a modern version of Solomon's judgment?*, Voelkerrechtsblog, 5 June 2019, available at: https://voelkerrechtsblog.org/the-charm-of-jurisdictions-a-modern-version-of-solomons-judgment/ (last accessed: 14 November 2021).

registered in the concerned state. The term 'shall' shows that this is an obligatory clause for all States parties. Further, jurisdiction is established regardless of the nationality or habitual residence of the victim or alleged perpetrator. Considering that alleged perpetrators might leave the country where the offence was committed if they are not residents or nationals, states are encouraged to develop legislation which authorizes them to issue international warrants of arrest and make use of the international collaboration networks such as INTERPOL.[322]

3.2.4.2 Art 4 (2) OPSC: Extraterritorial Jurisdiction

2. Each State Party may take such measures as may be necessary to establish its jurisdiction over the offences referred to in Article 3, paragraph 1, in the following cases:
   (a) When the alleged offender is a national of that State or a person who has his habitual residence in its territory;
   (b) When the victim is a national of that State.

Art 4 (2) regulates extraterritorial jurisdiction for OPSC offences. There are various approaches on how to establish extra-territorial jurisdiction. The most important component is the link to the asserting state, which can be established in different ways. For example, an asserting state justifies a link to its home country based on the nationality of either the offender ('active personality principle') or the victim ('passive personality principle').[323] The extra-territorial jurisdiction clause in the OPSC encompasses both the active and passive personality principle. Additionally, it extends the active personality principle to persons who merely have their habitual residence in the State party, without being citizens.[324] Unfortunately, the OPSC missed the opportunity to extend extraterritorial jurisdiction to victims who are not nationals, but residents of the asserting states. Considering the transnationality of the OPSC offences, maximum protection for survivors is key. Therefore, the CRC Committee encourages States parties to include such cases into their extra-territorial jurisdiction clauses.[325]

---

[322] CRC Committee, *Guidelines regarding the implementation of the Optional Protocol to the Convention on the Rights of the Child on the sale of children, child prostitution and child pornography*, CRC/C/156, paras. 80, 81.

[323] Gillespie, *Child Pornography. Law and Policy*, p. 304; Ryngaert, *Research Handbook on Jurisdiction and Immunities in International Law*, p. 51.

[324] Arguing that the assertion of jurisdiction over residents is in violation of international law, Danielle Ireland-Piper, *Extraterritorial Criminal Jurisdiction: Does the Long Arm of the Law Undermine the Rule of Law*, Melbourne Journal of International Law, Vol. 13 (2012), p. 131; Gillespie, *Child Pornography. Law and Policy*, pp. 305 et seq.

[325] CRC Committee, *Guidelines regarding the implementation of the Optional Protocol to the Convention on the Rights of the Child on the sale of children, child prostitution and child pornography*, CRC/C/156, paras. 82, 83; if more than one state claims jurisdiction, such jurisdictional conflict should be resolved through applying a best interests lens, see Sabine K. Witting, *Transnational by default: online child sexual abuse respects no borders*, International Journal of Children's Rights,

Acknowledging the challenges of territoriality associated with criminal offences committed with the support of ICT technologies, the CRC Committee encourages States parties to establish universal jurisdiction for all offences under the OPSC in order to 'put an end to the still widespread impunity for offences where there is no "hands-on" act'.[326] However, it is important to note that simply establishing universal jurisdiction will not solve the problem of transnational investigation and evidence collection as jurisdiction to adjudicate is different from jurisdiction to enforce. It must be recognised that the jurisdiction to investigate extra-territorially is not governed by Art 4 but can only be facilitated by formal and informal law enforcement collaboration mechanisms as set out in Arts 5 and 6: universal jurisdiction does not mean universal investigation.[327]

3.2.4.3 Art 4 (3) OPSC: Obligation to Prosecute Nationals under Specific Circumstances

> 3. Each State Party shall also take such measures as may be necessary to establish its jurisdiction over the above-mentioned offences when the alleged offender is present in its territory and it does not extradite him or her to another State Party on the ground that the offence has been committed by one of its nationals.

Art 4 (3) regulates that a state which does not want to extradite one of its citizens for an offence they committed abroad has to establish jurisdiction over this offence.[328] The clause effectively limits the optional character of Art 4(2), as it forces a State party to apply the active personality principle if it refuses to extradite one of its nationals.[329] Hereby, the clause again aims to close any loopholes in jurisdictional matters arising in transnational OPSC offences.

3.2.4.4 Art 4 (4) OPSC: Precedence of National Law

> 4. This Protocol does not exclude any criminal jurisdiction exercised in accordance with internal law.

Article 4(4) of the OPSC states that 'this Protocol does not exclude any criminal jurisdiction exercised in accordance with internal law'. This co-existence of

---

Vol. 29 (2021) and ACERWC, *General Comment No. 7 on Art 27 of the African Charter on the Rights and Welfare of the Child*, para. 94.

[326] CRC Committee, *Guidelines regarding the implementation of the Optional Protocol to the Convention on the Rights of the Child on the sale of children, child prostitution and child pornography*, CRC/C/156, para. 87.

[327] The CRC Committee indeed seems to conflate these two concepts, as the section on jurisdiction in the OPSC Guidelines refers to 'investigate and prosecute', see ibid., paras. 80 and 82.

[328] UNICEF Innocenti, *Handbook on the Optional Protocol on the Sale of Children, Child Prostitution and Child Pornography*, p. 13.

[329] Ibid.

jurisdiction based on international and national law reinforces the strong link between state sovereignty and jurisdiction, stressing the right of every state to regulate jurisdiction in its own way.

3.2.5 *Art 5 OPSC: Extradition*

Once a state has established its jurisdiction to adjudicate, it starts the investigation of the OPSC offence at hand. Extradition can be defined as 'the formal process by which one jurisdiction asks another for the enforced return of a person who is in the requested jurisdiction and who is accused or convicted of one or more criminal offences against the law of the requesting jurisdiction'.[330]

A problem for the smooth execution of extradition agreements is—apart from the fact that extradition treaties might not exist between the states—the so-called double criminality standard. The double criminality standard means that the conduct must be considered a criminal offence in both the requesting and the requested state.[331] This poses considerable challenges in the context of the OPSC, as the national criminal standards for these offences still differ. In response to this, the CRC Committee demands the abolishment of the double criminality standard for all offences criminalised under the OPSC.[332]

3.2.5.1 Art 5 (1) OPSC: Extradition Treaties

> 1. The offences referred to in article 3, paragraph 1, shall be deemed to be included as extraditable offences in any extradition treaty existing between States Parties and shall be included as extraditable offences in every extradition treaty subsequently concluded between them, in accordance with the conditions set forth in such treaties.

Art 5 (1) states that offences referred to in Art 3 (1) shall be considered extraditable offences in existing extradition treaties and be included as extraditable offences in future extradition treaties. The reference to Art 3 (1) shows that this should not apply to attempts to commit and complicity in committing 'child prostitution', sale of children and 'child pornography' offences, as this is regulated in Art 3 (2).[333]

---

[330] UNODC, *Manual on Mutual Legal Assistance and Extradition*, New York 2021, p. 41.

[331] Ibid., p. 69.

[332] CRC Committee, *Guidelines regarding the implementation of the Optional Protocol to the Convention on the Rights of the Child on the sale of children, child prostitution and child pornography*, CRC/C/156, para. 84–85; in comparison, Art 25 (4) Lanzarote Convention abolishes the double criminality requirement only for offences typically committed by travelling sex offenders.

[333] UNICEF Innocenti, *Handbook on the Optional Protocol on the Sale of Children, Child Prostitution and Child Pornography*, p. 14.

However, the CRC Committee encourages States parties to extend the application of extradition provisions to Art 3 (2) offences.[334]

3.2.5.2 Art 5 (2) OPSC: OPSC as Basis for Extradition

> 2. If a State Party that makes extradition conditional on the existence of a treaty receives a request for extradition from another State Party with which it has no extradition treaty, it may consider the present Protocol to be a legal basis for extradition in respect of such offences. Extradition shall be subject to the conditions provided by the law of the requested State.

Article 5 (2) of the OPSC provides that if a State party makes extradition dependent on the existence of an international treaty, the OPSC shall serve as the legal basis for such an extradition request. Even though the formulation 'it may consider' stresses that the requested state is not obligated to accept the OPSC as an extradition basis, it nonetheless gives states the opportunity to leverage the OPSC as an extradition basis, in line with the respective national law. Considering that especially online offences might force states which have no or limited diplomatic ties into collaboration, since the OPSC has 177 States parties,[335] this provision can facilitate extradition between these states, subject to their respective domestic legislation.

3.2.5.3 Art 5 (3) OPSC: Extradition without Need for Extradition Treaty

> 3. States Parties that do not make extradition conditional on the existence of a treaty shall recognize such offences as extraditable offences between themselves subject to the conditions provided by the law of the requested State.

Where a state does not make extradition dependent on the existence of a treaty, the state party should recognise Art 3 (1) offences as extraditable offences according to Art 5 (3). Even though it is phrased as a mandatory obligation ('shall recognize'), this is still subject to the 'conditions provided by the law of the requested State'. This should not be understood for national law to possibly circumvent this mandatory obligation. Rather, states have the opportunity to influence the exact procedure of the extradition process.[336]

---

[334] CRC Committee, *Guidelines regarding the implementation of the Optional Protocol to the Convention on the Rights of the Child on the sale of children, child prostitution and child pornography*, CRC/C/156, para. 89.

[335] For a full list of ratifications and accessions, see http://indicators.ohchr.org (last accessed: 19 November 2021).

[336] Tobin, *The Optional Protocol on the Sale of Children, Child Prostitution, and Child Pornography*, p. 1758.

3.2.5.4 Art 5 (4) OPSC: Fiction of *locus delicti*

> 4. Such offences shall be treated, for the purpose of extradition between States Parties, as if they had been committed not only in the place in which they occurred but also in the territories of the States required to establish their jurisdiction in accordance with article 4.

Art 5 (4) states that for the purpose of extradition, an OPSC offence will be treated as if it were committed in the territory of the requesting state, even if in fact it took place outside its territory. This fiction concerning the *locus delicti* serves to assist states in the extradition process, for which national law requires that the offence took place in the territory of the requesting state.[337]

3.2.5.5 Art 5 (5) OPSC: *aut dedere aut iudicare*

> 5. If an extradition request is made with respect to an offence described in article 3, paragraph 1, and the requested State Party does not or will not extradite on the basis of the nationality of the offender, that State shall take suitable measures to submit the case to its competent authorities for the purpose of prosecution.

Art 5 (5) is an expression of the so-called *aut dedere aut iudicare* principle, which requires that an offender should either be extradited to a requesting state or be prosecuted in the state in which they are present. Art 5 (5) needs to be read closely together with Art 4 (3), which requests states to prosecute one of its nationals if it refuses to extradite that person. Notably, Art 5 (5) depends on the condition 'if the request is made'. If no such request is made, a state could establish jurisdiction over one of its nationals in line with Art 4 (3) but refuse to take suitable measures to prosecute.[338] Considering the spirit of the OPSC to end impunity, this was most likely an unintended result of poor drafting. Therefore, even if no request is made, there should still be an obligation to prosecute a national offender.[339]

3.2.6 Art 6 OPSC: Mutual Legal Assistance

Art 6 regulates the States parties' responsibility in providing each other mutual legal assistance (hereafter MLA) in OPSC offences. Art 6 is *lex specialis* to Art 10, which speaks more generally about international collaboration and hence needs to be read together with Art 6. MLA in criminal matters is defined as 'a process by which States seek and provide assistance in gathering evidence for use in criminal cases'.

---

[337] Tobin, *The Optional Protocol on the Sale of Children, Child Prostitution, and Child Pornography*, p. 1758.
[338] Ibid.
[339] Ibid.

3.2.6.1 Art 6 (1): Greatest Measure of Assistance to Be Provided

> 1. States Parties shall afford one another the greatest measure of assistance in con-
> nection with investigations or criminal or extradition proceedings brought in respect
> of the offences set forth in article 3, paragraph 1, including assistance in obtaining
> evidence at their disposal necessary for the proceedings.

Art 6 (1) sets out the obligation of States parties to afford one another the 'greatest measure of assistance' in connection to the investigation of OPSC offences,
including the obligation to obtain evidence. Firstly, it must be noted that the obligation to provide MLA should also apply in cases of Art 3 (2). Further, the main
question is how the term 'greatest measure of assistance' is to be understood. This
should be generally interpreted as an obligation to undertake every possible effort
to assist another state.[340] However, this is much easier said than done. Considering
that an investigation on another state's territory usually requires the consent of
the affected state, formal processes in the area of MLA take a long time and are
cumbersome. It can take months and years to obtain crucial evidence needed for
an ongoing investigation.[341] As the OPSC offences often have an online element
to it, the collection of digital evidence becomes a key priority for cross-border
investigation. Taking the volatile nature of digital crime scenes into account, it is
questionable whether the generic provision of 'greatest measure of assistance' will
de facto assist law enforcement agencies with obtaining cross-border evidence.
Given that in online child sexual abuse cases the depicted child might be under
continuous threat of further abuse and exploitation, the situation places immense
pressure on law enforcement. The OPSC should therefore consider developing
comprehensive legal mechanisms tailored towards cross-border crime, including
digital crime scenes, such as the specific provisional MLA regulations complemented by a 24/7 network for speedy mutual assistance among parties set out in
the Budapest Convention (see section 2.2).[342] Otherwise, the MLA mechanism in
the OPSC might lose its relevance.

3.2.6.2 Art 6 (2): Assistance in Conformity with Other Treaties and Domestic Law

> 2. States Parties shall carry out their obligations under paragraph 1 of the present arti-
> cle in conformity with any treaties or other arrangements on mutual legal assistance

---

[340] Tobin, *The Optional Protocol on the Sale of Children, Child Prostitution, and Child Pornography,*
p. 1760.

[341] Philip J. Pullen, *Nail in the MLAT Coffin: Examining Alternatives Solutions to the Current Mutual
Legal Assistance Treaty Regime in International Cross-Border Data Sharing,* North Carolina Journal of
International Law, Vol. 44 (2018), p. 4; Jean-Baptiste Maillart, *The limits of subjective territorial juris-
diction in the context of cybercrime,* ERA Forum 2019, p. 384; Osula, *Mutual Legal Assistance & Other
Mechanisms for Accessing Extraterritorially Located Data,* p. 51.

[342] See Arts 27–34 Budapest Convention.

that may exist between them. In the absence of such treaties or arrangements, States Parties shall afford one another assistance in accordance with their domestic law.

Art 6 (2) further qualifies the generic obligation of States parties set out under Art 6 (1). It requests States parties to conduct any MLA collaboration in line with existing MLA treaties and in the absence of such treaties, they should afford each other MLA in line with their national laws. Like extradition, MLA is in many countries governed by a two-pronged system comprising national legislation and bi- or multilateral treaties.[343] While national legislation sets out the domestic procedure for facilitating the requests, many countries require a bi- or multilateral treaty regulating and legitimising such requests at a transnational level with the requesting or receiving state.[344] However, even if national law requires an international treaty between requesting and requested state to provide MLA, the obligation under Art 6 (1) should not be rendered inapplicable. States parties should 'contribute in any way possible to facilitating investigations in their territory',[345] for example through informal MLA, or by working towards drafting an MLA treaty with the requesting state.[346]

3.2.7 Art 7 OPSC: Seizure and Confiscation

States Parties shall, subject to the provisions of their national law:
    (a) Take measures to provide for the seizure and confiscation, as appropriate, of:
        (i) Goods, such as materials, assets and other instrumentalities used to commit or facilitate offences under the present protocol;
        (ii) Proceeds derived from such offences;
    (b) Execute requests from another State Party for seizure or confiscation of goods or proceeds referred to in subparagraph (a);
    (c) Take measures aimed at closing, on a temporary or definitive basis, premises used to commit such offences.

Art 7 requires States parties to seize and confiscate any goods used to commit or facilitate offences, or proceeds derived from such offence, and close down any premises used to commit OPSC offences.[347] Like in Arts 5 and 6, Art 7 does not

---

[343] UNODC, *Manual on Mutual Legal Assistance and Extradition*, pp. 21–22.

[344] Ibid., pp. 21–22; if there is no treaty in place, a requesting country is entirely dependent on the willingness of the requested law enforcement authority, see Jan-Jaap Oerlemans, *Investigating cybercrime*, Amsterdam 2017, p. 63.

[345] CRC Committee, *Guidelines regarding the implementation of the Optional Protocol to the Convention on the Rights of the Child on the sale of children, child prostitution and child pornography*, CRC/C/156, para. 108.

[346] For alternatives to formal MLA requests, see UNODC, *Manual on Mutual Legal Assistance and Extradition*, pp. 65 et seq.

[347] CRC Committee, *Guidelines regarding the implementation of the Optional Protocol to the Convention on the Rights of the Child on the sale of children, child prostitution and child pornography*, CRC/C/156, para. 74.

make references to attempts, complicity and participation but should neverthe-less also apply in these cases. Further, the seizure and confiscation regime under the OPSC is 'subject to the provisions of their national law'. This should not be understood to give States parties the opportunities to escape their obligation under the OPSC: domestic law will regulate the *how*, not the *if* of seizure and con-fiscation procedures.

In the context of online child sexual abuse offences, an additional challenge is that the material itself can become the currency. Instead of making a payment in exchange for child sexual abuse material, the material is traded against other material.[348] This makes it more difficult for law enforcement to detect patterns of commercial online child sexual abuse and exploitation. Further, offenders are increasingly using cryptocurrencies to pay for child sexual abuse material online, with an increase of 212 % from 2017 to 2019 in Bitcoin and Ethereum payments linked to addresses offering child sexual abuse material.[349] Even though it is possible to trace such payments, not all law enforcements will have the techni-cal expertise and equipment to do so.[350] This poses additional challenges for the implementation of Art 7.

3.2.8   *Art 8 OPSC: Child-Friendly Justice*

Art 8 sets out the rights and protections of child victims of OPSC offences in the criminal justice system. The successful investigation and prosecution of OPSC offences is an important aspect in the rehabilitation of the victim and hence closely linked to Art 9 (3).[351] The CRC Committee recommends an interpretation of Art 8 in line with the Guidelines on Justice in Matters involving Child Victims and Witnesses of Crime[352] (hereafter: Child Justice Guidelines).[353] Even though Art 8 and the Child Justice Guidelines are tailored towards children in contact with the criminal justice system, the CRC Committee recommends a *mutatis mutandis*

---

[348] UNODC, *Study on the Effects of New Information Technologies on the Abuse of Children*, p. 18; highlighting the increasing importance of self-generated child sexual abuse material as currency, WeProtect Global Alliance, *Global Threat Assessment 2021*, p. 54.

[349] WeProtect Global Alliance, *Global Threat Assessment 2021*, p. 52; ICMEC, *Cryptocurrency and the trade of online child sexual abuse material*, Virginia 2021.

[350] WeProtect Global Alliance, *Global Threat Assessment 2021*, p. 62.

[351] CRC Committee, *Guidelines regarding the implementation of the Optional Protocol to the Convention on the Rights of the Child on the sale of children, child prostitution and child pornography*, CRC/C/156, para. 107.

[352] UN Economic and Social Council, *Guidelines on Justice in Matters involving Child Victims and Witnesses of Crime*, E/CN.15/2005/L.2/Ref.1.

[353] CRC Committee, *Guidelines regarding the implementation of the Optional Protocol to the Convention on the Rights of the Child on the sale of children, child prostitution and child pornography*, CRC/C/156, para. 91.

application for children in contact with administrative and civil proceedings.[354] Considering that the Child Justice Guidelines extend the definition of 'justice process' to customary and informal justice systems,[355] the same should apply in the context of Art 8. Lastly, it should be acknowledged that there are various paths for children to seek justice, and that especially for violations committed in the digital environment, the possibility of collective complaints, including class actions and strategic litigation, should be considered.[356]

3.2.8.1 Art 8 (1): Protection of Rights and Interests of Child Victim

1. States Parties shall adopt appropriate measures to protect the rights and interests of child victims of the practices prohibited under the present Protocol at all stages of the criminal justice process, in particular by:
(a) Recognizing the vulnerability of child victims and adapting procedures to recognize their special needs, including their special needs as witnesses;

Art 8 (1) sets out the appropriate measures States parties shall adopt to protect child victims of OPSC offences at all stages of the criminal justice process. As a first measure, Art 8 (1) (a) requires States parties to recognise the vulnerability of child victims and to provide for special procedures which recognise the special needs of child victims and witnesses. This needs to be understood to apply to two stages: firstly, the child needs to be able to easily access the criminal justice system, and secondly, once in the criminal justice system, the focus needs to be on establishing child-friendly and gender-sensitive procedures and services which avoid secondary trauma to the child victim.

To facilitate children's access to the criminal justice systems, States parties should offer a variety of reporting mechanisms, which should be regulated by law and clearly define the referral pathway for reported cases. This should also include telephonic and online reporting mechanisms, as well as the opportunity to report anonymously.[357] Further, states should endeavour to establish so-called one-stop centres, in which child survivors receive all relevant services in one location, including legal, counselling, medical and other relevant services.[358] This increases the efficiency of the response as the child does not need to seek services in various

---

354 CRC Committee, *Guidelines regarding the implementation of the Optional Protocol to the Convention on the Rights of the Child on the sale of children, child prostitution and child pornography,* CRC/C/156, para. 99.

355 UN Economic and Social Council, *Guidelines on Justice in Matters involving Child Victims and Witnesses of Crime,* E/CN.15/2005/L.2/Ref.1, para. 9.

356 CRC Committee, *General comment No. 25 (2021) on children's rights in relation to the digital environment,* CRC/C/GC/25, para. 44.

357 CRC Committee, *Guidelines regarding the implementation of the Optional Protocol to the Convention on the Rights of the Child on the sale of children, child prostitution and child pornography,* CRC/C/156, para. 96.

358 Ibid.

locations, which might be a deterrent to report a case in the first place and also adds unnecessary travel costs, which children from poor backgrounds often times cannot afford.

In the context of COVID-19, courts in many countries were closed for a considerable period or limited to urgent appeals, which often did not cover OPSC offences. In this context, countries started increasing the use of virtual courts to ensure access to justice for children even in times of lockdown or movement restrictions.[359] In the same vein, the operationalisation of mobile courts brings the formal justice system directly into the children's communities.[360] Both virtual and mobile courts therefore aim to assist children to overcome the geographical boundaries of accessing the criminal justice systems.

Another *de lege* hurdle of access to justice for child victims of OPSC offences are statutory limitations for OPSC offences. Statutory limitations refer to a period after which criminal proceedings cannot be instituted anymore. Survivors of OPSC offences often report such offences years after they occurred due to a feeling of guilt, shame or fear. Therefore, the CRC Committee recommends abolishing statutory limitations altogether, and where this is not feasible, they should only start to run once the survivor turns 18 years old.[361]

Regarding the establishment of child-friendly and gender-sensitive criminal procedures, States parties are obliged to create an enabling environment which avoids secondary traumatisation of the child victim by any means necessary.[362] Forensic interviews should be conducted in a child-friendly environment using evidence-based protocols. Avoiding multiple interviews with the child is equally important, as otherwise the child might be under the impression that they are not being believed.[363] Testimonial aids, such as anatomically correct dolls, can further be helpful to assist the child in expressing itself.[364] Overall, interference with the

---

[359] For example in Bangladesh, see UNICEF, *Access to Justice for Children in the era of COVID-19: Notes from the Field*, New York 2020, p. 41.

[360] UNICEF, *#Reimagine Justice for Children*, New York 2021, p. 5.

[361] CRC Committee, *Guidelines regarding the implementation of the Optional Protocol to the Convention on the Rights of the Child on the sale of children, child prostitution and child pornography*, CRC/C/156, para. 95.

[362] As stipulated in the context of child rights violations in the digital environment, see CRC Committee, *General comment No. 25 (2021) on children's rights in relation to the digital environment*, CRC/C/GC/25, para. 45.

[363] CRC Committee, *Guidelines regarding the implementation of the Optional Protocol to the Convention on the Rights of the Child on the sale of children, child prostitution and child pornography*, CRC/C/156, para. 97; UN Economic and Social Council, *Guidelines on Justice in Matters involving Child Victims and Witnesses of Crime*, E/CN.15/2005/L.2/Ref.1, para. 31.

[364] UN Economic and Social Council, *Guidelines on Justice in Matters involving Child Victims and Witnesses of Crime*, E/CN.15/2005/L.2/Ref.1, para. 31.

child's right to privacy should be limited, while ensuring that highest standards of evidence collection are upheld.[365] A key component to avoid re-traumatisation of the child in the court room environment is to avoid direct confrontation between the child and the accused. Depending on the country context, suitable measures may reach from using a CCTV system connected to a separate witness room, to one-way mirrors between witness room and court room, or simply alternating the presence between child and accused in the court room.[366] The use of CCTV systems is particularly important if the child is participating in a transnational OPSC case. Travelling to the country where the trial takes place can be very uprooting for the child and hence negatively impact the child's rehabilitation and reintegration. Participating virtually is therefore the most suitable solution from a best interests of the child perspective.[367] At the same time, CCTV systems should be used with caution in cases where digital means, such as cameras, were involved in the abuse of the child.[368] In these cases, the suitability of the use of such measures should be discussed with the child in an age-appropriate manner.

Further, corroborative evidence, such as crime scene evidence, including DNA evidence, are key to support the child's testimony.[369] Evidentiary rules, such as a prohibition of introducing the victim's sexual history as evidence, or the abolishment of cautionary rules in relation to child witnesses, also play an important role in creating a safe court environment for child victims.[370] Access to relevant evidence such as child sexual abuse material should be heavily restricted while respecting fair trial principles.[371] In addition, the CRC Committee recommends the use of pre-recorded videos of forensic interviews with the child as evidence in

---

[365] UN Economic and Social Council, *Guidelines on Justice in Matters involving Child Victims and Witnesses of Crime*, E/CN.15/2005/L.2/Ref.1, para. 12.

[366] CRC Committee, *Guidelines regarding the implementation of the Optional Protocol to the Convention on the Rights of the Child on the sale of children, child prostitution and child pornography*, CRC/C/156, para. 97; UN Economic and Social Council, *Guidelines on Justice in Matters involving Child Victims and Witnesses of Crime*, E/CN.15/2005/L.2/Ref., para. 31.

[367] For further discussion on the best interests of the child principle in transnational court procedures, see Witting, *Transnational by default: online child sexual abuse respects no borders, International Journal of Children's Rights*.

[368] ECPAT, *Explanatory Report to the Guidelines Regarding the Implementation of the Optional Protocol to the Convention on the Rights of the Child on the Sale of Children, Child Prostitution and Child Pornography*, p. 94.

[369] CRC Committee, *Guidelines regarding the implementation of the Optional Protocol to the Convention on the Rights of the Child on the sale of children, child prostitution and child pornography*, CRC/C/156, para. 94.

[370] Stating that a child's testimony should not be considered invalid or untrustworthy merely because it was given by a child, UN Economic and Social Council, *Guidelines on Justice in Matters involving Child Victims and Witnesses of Crime*, E/CN.15/2005/L.2/Ref.1, para. 18.

[371] ECPAT, *Explanatory Report to the Guidelines Regarding the Implementation of the Optional Protocol to the Convention on the Rights of the Child on the Sale of Children, Child Prostitution and Child Pornography*, p. 94.

court.[372] Even though this might in theory replace the need for an *in persona* testimony, pre-recorded videos also carry the risk of exposing the interview technique to extreme scrutiny by the defence. If the interviewer is not sufficiently trained and experienced in interviewing child victims, there is a considerable risk that the interviewer might use leading questions or make other mistakes which from an evidential perspective can negatively influence the child's credibility.

Lastly, the CRC Committee requires States parties to take additional precautionary measures to protect the child's interests when the accused is caregiver, family member, or another child.[373]

> (b) Informing child victims of their rights, their role and the scope, timing and progress of the proceedings and of the disposition of their cases;

The child's right to be informed of their rights, their role, the status of the proceedings and the disposition of their cases is a key element of a child-friendly justice system.[374] Child survivors of OPSC might often feel a sense of not being in control of their own lives, as they have been robbed of this control and agency by the violence they experienced. Keeping the child informed at all stages of the criminal trial is therefore key to ensure the child is at the centre of the proceedings. It is essential that the child is informed in a language that the child understands, in an age-appropriate manner and taking any other vulnerabilities such as disabilities into account.[375] This right is granted to every child who participates in the criminal justice process, regardless of whether the child has legal capacity or not.[376]

> (c) Allowing the views, needs and concerns of child victims to be presented and considered in proceedings where their personal interests are affected, in a manner consistent with the procedural rules of national law;

Closely linked to the right to be informed under Art 8 (1) (b), is the right to be heard set out in Art 8 (1) (c). It requires States parties to ensure that the views

---

[372] ECPAT, *Explanatory Report to the Guidelines Regarding the Implementation of the Optional Protocol to the Convention on the Rights of the Child on the Sale of Children, Child Prostitution and Child Pornography*, p. 91.

[373] CRC Committee, *Guidelines regarding the implementation of the Optional Protocol to the Convention on the Rights of the Child on the sale of children, child prostitution and child pornography*, CRC/C/156, para. 97.

[374] UN Economic and Social Council, *Guidelines on Justice in Matters involving Child Victims and Witnesses of Crime*, E/CN.15/2005/L.2/Ref.1, paras. 19–20.

[375] CRC Committee, *Guidelines regarding the implementation of the Optional Protocol to the Convention on the Rights of the Child on the sale of children, child prostitution and child pornography*, CRC/C/156, para. 92; see also WeProtect Global Alliance, *The Sexual exploitation and abuse of deaf and disabled children*, available here: https://www.weprotect.org/wp-content/uploads/Intelligence-briefing-2021-The-sexual-exploitation-and-abuse-of-disabled-children.pdf (last accessed: 24 April 2022).

[376] Ibid.

and concerns of a child victim are considered in proceedings where their personal interests are affected, in line with national procedural law.[377] This right is closely linked to Art 12 CRC and even exceeds this protection standard as it is not restricted to a child 'who is capable of forming his or her own views' and allows for the child's voice to be heard through the assistance of third parties, such as parents, social workers or intermediaries.[378] Naturally, the child should be free to choose the language in which their views are raised. Depending on the national legal system, the child should also benefit from free legal aid and be supported by a lawyer in expressing their views.[379]

Apart from being given the opportunity to speak as a witness, there are two important ways to give child victims the opportunity to be heard and take a special role in the criminal proceedings. The first one is so-called victim impact statements, which are usually produced by the prosecution during sentencing stage. These written or oral statements give the child victim the opportunity to directly address the court and explain the impact the crime had on them. A recent example of the weight victim impact statements can have during sentencing stage is the case of the former Team USA gymnastics doctor referred to under section 3.2.2.2 where one of his victims, Kyle Stephens, addressed her abuser directly with the iconic words:

> Perhaps you have figured it out by now, but little girls don't stay little forever. They grow into strong women who return to destroy your world.[380]

Stephens reported later that it was 'really empowering to get up there and give my story from start to finish.'[381] As many child survivors of sexual abuse and exploitation are robbed of their agency, victim impact statements can be an important part in the healing process to regain this agency over their own body and life.

Another opportunity to actively participate in the court process are private accessory prosecutions. Even though the exact model varies from country to country, the idea behind accessory prosecutions is that victims, with support from a lawyer, can join the public prosecutor as an additional party in the trial with clear and far-reaching rights, like the right to put questions, right to move for the admission of

[377] UN Economic and Social Council, *Guidelines on Justice in Matters involving Child Victims and Witnesses of Crime*, E/CN.15/2005/L.2/Ref.1, para. 21.
[378] Tobin, *The Optional Protocol on the Sale of Children, Child Prostitution, and Child Pornography*, p. 1766.
[379] CRC Committee, *Guidelines regarding the implementation of the Optional Protocol to the Convention on the Rights of the Child on the sale of children, child prostitution and child pornography*, CRC/C/156, para. 97.
[380] BBC, *Larry Nassar case: The 156 women who confronted a predator*, 25 January 2018, available here: https://www.bbc.com/news/world-us-canada-42725339 (last accessed: 14 June 2022).
[381] Ibid.

evidence, right to participate in the final argument and even the right to appeal.[382] Such a model gives victims of violent crimes, including sexual offences, the opportunity for active participation which can considerably contribute to their healing process.

(d) Providing appropriate support services to child victims throughout the legal process;

Art 8 1) (d) requires States parties to provide appropriate support services throughout the entire legal process. Even though the exact type of services is not specified, this should include the full range of multisectoral support services including legal, medical, social welfare, psychological, psychiatric and any other expertise which might improve the overall wellbeing of the child victim.[383] While the child friendly procedures during the criminal trial as set out in Art 8 1) (a) are key to protect the child from secondary trauma, equally important are pre-trial preparation and post-trial care. Pre-trial preparation aims to familiarise the child with the court room, the role of the different actors in the court room, and the prosecutor and other support staff working on the specific case. Post-trial care is aimed at supporting the healing of the child, including the processing of the experiences of the criminal justice process.[384]

(e) Protecting, as appropriate, the privacy and identity of child victims and taking measures in accordance with national law to avoid the inappropriate dissemination of information that could lead to the identification of child victims;

The child's privacy is a key element for creating a conducive court environment where the child feels protected enough to freely speak about the violence they have experienced. Knowing that this information does not leave the court room and will not be publicly accessible is at the centre of the child's right to privacy. Court cases involving OPSC offences should therefore be held in closed chambers, in accordance with national law. While it is important that the media informs the public about OPSC cases, considerable efforts need to be undertaken to ensure that no information about the child's identity is disclosed to the general public.[385] Media guidelines for ethical reporting on violence cases involving child victims

---

[382] See for example Germany, Criminal Procedure Act, paras. 395 et seq, available here: https://www.gesetze-im-internet.de/englisch_stpo/index.html (last accessed: 6 December 2021).

[383] CRC Committee, *Guidelines regarding the implementation of the Optional Protocol to the Convention on the Rights of the Child on the sale of children, child prostitution and child pornography*, CRC/C/156, para. 97; UN Economic and Social Council, *Guidelines on Justice in Matters involving Child Victims and Witnesses of Crime*, E/CN.15/2005/L.2/Ref.1, paras. 22 et seq.

[384] CRC Committee, *Guidelines regarding the implementation of the Optional Protocol to the Convention on the Rights of the Child on the sale of children, child prostitution and child pornography*, CRC/C/156, para. 100.

[385] Ibid., para. 28; UN Economic and Social Council, *Guidelines on Justice in Matters involving Child Victims and Witnesses of Crime*, E/CN.15/2005/L.2/Ref., paras. 26–28.

should be developed to ensure media reporting follows the best interests of the child principle.[386]

(f) Providing, in appropriate cases, for the safety of child victims, as well as that of their families and witnesses on their behalf, from intimidation and retaliation;

Child victims of OPSC offences might be exposed to intimidation and retaliation. If the child was violated in the context of organised crime, the child might be exposed to serious threats to stop the child from participating in the criminal justice process. If the child was violated by a family or community member, the child might be pressurised to stop participation in the justice process due to the fear of losing face or bringing 'shame' over the family.

To make the safety of the child victim the utmost priority, a risk assessment needs to be conducted upon the first contact with the justice system.[387] The risk assessment then needs to be constantly reviewed to ensure appropriate protective measures are taken. Such measures can include restraining orders, pre-trial detention of the accused or setting special 'no contact' bail conditions, or putting a child victim under witness protection.[388]

The OPSC limits this provision to 'appropriate cases', without specifying this term further. Therefore, States parties have the discretion to determine when special protection measures are indeed necessary. To ensure that the qualification as 'appropriate case' is reassessed on a regular basis, the ongoing and repeated risk assessment should be considered a minimum standard.

(g) Avoiding unnecessary delay in the disposition of cases and the execution of orders or decrees granting compensation to child victims.

The OPSC requires States parties to avoid any unnecessary delays in the adjudication of OPSC offences. The speediness of the justice process is one of the core principles of child-friendly justice.[389] In order to meet this standard, the CRC Committee recommends the fast tracking of OPSC cases.[390] It further notes that delays should only be approved after consultation with the affected child.[391] On

---

[386] See for example Terre des Hommes, *Child Safeguarding Guidance for Journalists*, September 2014.

[387] Tobin, *The Optional Protocol on the Sale of Children, Child Prostitution, and Child Pornography*, p. 1768.

[388] UN Economic and Social Council, *Guidelines on Justice in Matters involving Child Victims and Witnesses of Crime*, E/CN.15/2005/L.2/Ref.1, paras. 32–34.

[389] Ibid., para. 30.

[390] CRC Committee, *Guidelines regarding the implementation of the Optional Protocol to the Convention on the Rights of the Child on the sale of children, child prostitution and child pornography*, CRC/C/156, para. 98.

[391] Ibid.

the other hand, delays can be acceptable if they serve the best interests of the child.[392]

Art 8 1) (g) gained significant importance during the COVID-19 pandemic, where courts were closed for a considerable period. Countries advocated for courts to be recognised as essential services and for children's cases to be prioritised.[393]

3.2.8.2 Art 8 (2): Uncertainty regarding Age of Child Victim

> 2. States Parties shall ensure that uncertainty as to the actual age of the victim shall not prevent the initiation of criminal investigations, including investigations aimed at establishing the age of the victim.

Legal identity documents such as birth certificates are an important pre-condition for many children to access the justice system. If they do not have such documents, they might either not be considered a 'child' as their age is not clear, or they might not be considered citizens. States parties therefore should ensure that all children, even the ones without legal identity documents, can enjoy legal protection.[394]

Particularly vulnerable are children in migration or children in street situations. In such cases, age assessments are often conducted to determine the age of the child. States parties are obliged to conduct age assessments in a 'safe, child and gender-sensitive and fair manner', and not only rely on physical appearance, but also take the psychological maturity into account.[395] As age assessment methods might not always provide an exact age, States parties should grant persons the benefit of the doubt and treat them as children when no conclusive results can be reached.[396] This was confirmed in a recent case brought against Spain regarding an age assessment of an unaccompanied minor, where the CRC Committee stated that 'X-ray evidence lacks precision, has a wide margin of error and is therefore unsuitable for use as the sole method of assessing the chronological age of a young person who claims to be a minor'. Further, the Committee took a very clear stance on age assessment methods which are found to violate children's rights: 'tests that are conducted to determine the age of a child and that involve nudity,

---

[392] UN Economic and Social Council, *Guidelines on Justice in Matters involving Child Victims and Witnesses of Crime*, E/CN.15/2005/L.2/Ref.1, para. 30.

[393] UNICEF, *Access to Justice for Children in the era of COVID-19: Notes from the Field*, p. 24.

[394] ECPAT, *Explanatory Report to the Guidelines Regarding the Implementation of the Optional Protocol to the Convention on the Rights of the Child on the Sale of Children, Child Prostitution and Child Pornography*, p. 87.

[395] CRC Committee, *General Comment No. 6 (2005) Treatment of unaccompanied and separated children outside the country of their origin*, CRC/GC/2005/6 (1 September 2005), para. 31.

[396] CRC Committee, *Views adopted by the Committee under the Optional Protocol to the Convention on the Rights of the Child on a communications procedure, concerning communication No. 76/2019*, CRC/C/86/D/76/2019 (2021), para. 8.6.

or an examination of genitalia or other intimate parts of the body violate a child's dignity, privacy and bodily integrity and should be prohibited'.[397]

3.2.8.3 Art 8 (3): Best Interest of Child Victim

3. States Parties shall ensure that, in the treatment by the criminal justice system of children who are victims of the offences described in the present Protocol, the best interest of the child shall be a primary consideration.

In line with Art 3 CRC, the Committee requires States parties to make the best interests of the child victim a primary consideration in the criminal justice process. Giving the child sufficient time to receive support before getting involved in the criminal justice system, especially in cases of intra-family abuse, is an expression of the best interests of the child principle in this context.[398] Further, the justice system should ensure that the time of the day for the interview, the length of each interview session and the overall length of the interview process are in line with the child's level of maturity and development.[399] In summary, any measures which follow the principles of child-friendly justice, such as the ones discussed in Art 8 (1), ultimately serve the best interests of the child.[400] The words 'shall ensure' place a strong legal obligation on States parties. It is important to note that Art 8 (3), just like Art 3 CRC, makes the child's best interests 'a primary consideration'. This gives States parties a certain flexibility as to how this principle is applied. However, at a minimum, the child's best interest carries significant weight in any conflict as the expression 'a primary consideration' means that it 'may not be considered on the same level as all other considerations'.[401]

3.2.8.4 Art 8 (4) Training

4. States Parties shall take measures to ensure appropriate training, in particular legal and psychological training, for the persons who work with victims of the offences prohibited under the present Protocol.

---

[397] CRC Committee, *Views adopted by the Committee under the Optional Protocol to the Convention on the Rights of the Child on a communications procedure, concerning communication No. 76/2019*, CRC/C/86/D/76/2019 (2021), para. 8.8.

[398] CRC Committee, *Guidelines regarding the implementation of the Optional Protocol to the Convention on the Rights of the Child on the sale of children, child prostitution and child pornography*, CRC/C/156, para. 93.

[399] ECPAT, *Explanatory Report to the Guidelines Regarding the Implementation of the Optional Protocol to the Convention on the Rights of the Child on the Sale of Children, Child Prostitution and Child Pornography*, p. 88.

[400] CRC Committee, *Guidelines regarding the implementation of the Optional Protocol to the Convention on the Rights of the Child on the sale of children, child prostitution and child pornography*, CRC/C/156, para. 97.

[401] CRC Committee, *General comment No. 14 (2013) on the right of the child to have his or her best interests taken as a primary consideration (art. 3, para. 1)*, CRC/C/GC/14 (29 May 2013), p. 6.

Training for multi-sectoral stakeholders is a key intervention to realise the rights of child victims and avoid any secondary trauma.[402] Considering the psychological impact working with OPSC survivors can have on professionals, the duty of care requires that they are at least provided with comprehensive training to fulfil these duties.[403] It is hereby important to not only focus on the primary service providers in the response to such offences, but also on frontline workers who are in the position to identify and refer cases of OPSC offences.[404] This naturally includes professionals who spend a considerable amount of time with children and might be considered a trusted adult for the child, such as educators, teachers, health professionals and coaches.[405] These professionals need to be trained in identifying signs of OPSC offences, understanding child development, disclosure processes, trauma impact and understanding victim-perpetrator relationships. They further need to be capacitated to respond to disclosures of OPSC offences in a child- and gender sensitive manner.[406]

For the criminal justice sector response, dedicated training for police, prosecution, judiciary, social workers and intermediaries are required to respond to child victims in a child-centred and gender-sensitive manner.[407] The upholding of the best interest principle set out in Art 8 (3) takes centre stage. Such trainings should include dedicated modules on online-facilitated OPSC offences, including the use of online tools for the investigation and victim identification.[408]

---

[402] UN Economic and Social Council, *Guidelines on Justice in Matters involving Child Victims and Witnesses of Crime*, E/CN.15/2005/L.2/Ref.1, para. 43.

[403] ECPAT, *Explanatory Report to the Guidelines Regarding the Implementation of the Optional Protocol to the Convention on the Rights of the Child on the Sale of Children, Child Prostitution and Child Pornography*, p. 42.

[404] CRC Committee, *Guidelines regarding the implementation of the Optional Protocol to the Convention on the Rights of the Child on the sale of children, child prostitution and child pornography*, CRC/C/156, para. 29.

[405] ECPAT, *Explanatory Report to the Guidelines Regarding the Implementation of the Optional Protocol to the Convention on the Rights of the Child on the Sale of Children, Child Prostitution and Child Pornography*, p. 43.

[406] CRC Committee, *Guidelines regarding the implementation of the Optional Protocol to the Convention on the Rights of the Child on the sale of children, child prostitution and child pornography*, CRC/C/156, para. 30.

[407] Ibid.

[408] Ibid., para. 39.

Training developers should aim to collaborate with survivor advocacy groups.[409]
Their role is crucial in giving a face to these offences and educate professionals on
the complexities of OPSC offences and their long-term impact on survivors.[410]

Lastly, to measure the effectiveness of trainings, their impact on the daily practice
of professionals should be regularly evaluated.[411]

3.2.8.5 Art 8 (5) Witness Protection Programmes

> 5. States Parties shall, in appropriate cases, adopt measures in order to protect the
> safety and integrity of those persons and/or organizations involved in the prevention
> and/or protection and rehabilitation of victims of such offences.

Art 8 (5) is closely linked to the obligation under Art 8 1) (f). However, while the
latter is narrower by focusing on the protection of child witnesses and their families from retaliation and intimidation, the former creates an obligation to protect
any persons or organisations involved in the protection or rehabilitation of child
survivors. This obligation is therefore not limited to the criminal justice process
or to persons directly involved in its proceedings.[412] Considering that the term
'appropriate case' is not further defined, States parties have discretion regarding
the definition of this term.

3.2.8.6 Art 8 (6): Non-prejudice to Fair Trial Principles

> 6. Nothing in the present Article shall be construed as prejudicial to or inconsistent
> with the rights of the accused to a fair and impartial trial.

Art 8 (6) clarifies that none of the provisions on Art 8 should be construed to prejudice the accused's right to a fair trial. The right to a fair trial is anchored in Art 14
International Covenant on Civil and Political Rights, with a dedicated expression
for child offenders in Art 37 and 40 CRC. While Art 8 (5) therefore only reinforces
the fair trial principles set out in other international treaties, the reminder of the
fair trial principles is crucial in the context of the OPSC offences. A violation of

---

[409] ECPAT, *Explanatory Report to the Guidelines Regarding the Implementation of the Optional
Protocol to the Convention on the Rights of the Child on the Sale of Children, Child Prostitution and Child
Pornography*, p. 42.

[410] For a list of survivor advocacy groups in the context of online child sexual abuse and exploitation, see the compilation by the Canadian Centre for Child Protection here: https://protectchildren
.ca/en/programs-and-initiatives/survivor-advocacy-groups/ (last accessed: 10 Dec 2021).

[411] CRC Committee, *Guidelines regarding the implementation of the Optional Protocol to the
Convention on the Rights of the Child on the sale of children, child prostitution and child pornography*,
CRC/C/156, para. 29.

[412] Tobin, *The Optional Protocol on the Sale of Children, Child Prostitution, and Child Pornography*,
p. 1772.

children's rights, especially through abuse and exploitation, often sparks a public outcry and asks for the perpetrators to be brought to book, no matter what it takes. The OPSC in this context therefore reminds us that despite the horrific offences set out in the OPSC, the fair trial principle shall not be violated. Where the fair trial principle is limited, a proportionate balance must be upheld between the best interests of the child principle reinforced under Art 8 (3) and fair trial principles. This includes issues such as delaying the start of the trial to give the child time to recover, but also interviewing children outside the courtroom and allowing this interview record as admissible evidence in the trial.[413]

In the context of fair trial principles, the CRC Committee also reminds States parties that children who commit OPSC offences should be treated differently from adults by diverting them from the criminal justice system towards therapeutic services.[414]

3.2.9 Art 9 OPSC: Prevention, Rehabilitation, and Compensation

3.2.9.1 Art 9 (1): Preventative Measures

> 1. States Parties shall adopt or strengthen, implement and disseminate laws, administrative measures, social policies and programmes to prevent the offences referred to in the present Protocol. Particular attention shall be given to protect children who are especially vulnerable to these practices.

Art 9 (1) requires States parties to conceptualise and implement various measures, including laws, administrative measures, social policies, and other programmes to prevent the OPSC offences, with a focus on particularly vulnerable children. Even though the OPSC does not specify the exact measures, the CRC Committee in its Guidelines spells out various recommendations on how both the demand and the supply side of sale and sexual exploitation of children can be curtailed.

Firstly, the Committee requires member states to develop strategies which address underlying causes which enable OPSC offences.[415] In many States parties, social tolerance towards violence against children exists and ending this practice is

---

[413] ECPAT, *Explanatory Report to the Guidelines Regarding the Implementation of the Optional Protocol to the Convention on the Rights of the Child on the Sale of Children, Child Prostitution and Child Pornography*, p. 90.

[414] CRC Committee, *Guidelines regarding the implementation of the Optional Protocol to the Convention on the Rights of the Child on the sale of children, child prostitution and child pornography*, CRC/C/156, para. 71.

[415] Ibid., para. 32.

perceived as beyond the control of communities to change.[416] Paired with non-appreciation for children as rights holders, and harmful beliefs around sexuality and masculinity, including sexual entitlement among perpetrators, creates an environment where children are vulnerable to OPSC offences.[417]

Considering the patriarchal root causes described above, the CRC Committee makes it clear that prevention strategies need to apply a gender perspective.[418] Patriarchal societies create twofold dynamics of violence, which also affect children. Firstly, members of the privileged group use violence towards the 'subordinate' group to sustain their dominance and secondly, violence is important in gender politics amongst men by using violence to make exclusions towards non-gender compliant men.[419] Applying this to the gender-specific vulnerabilities of children, girls will experience violence as part of the non-dominant group whose subordination needs to be maintained. Boys might experience violence either because they are children and hence considered subordinate, or because they do not conform with the predominant narrative of masculinity and are punished for that (and often labelled 'gay' in the process). This gendered violence boys experience in their childhood might then translate into exercising violence over others, in order to regain power and manifest dominance. The societal pressure to conform with masculine expectations hence plays a crucial role in displaying violent behaviour later in life.[420] These gender perspectives are crucial to prevent violence against children and break the cycle of intergenerational violence. Harmful gender stereotypes are further reproduced in the regulation of sexual offences. Criminal law is often infused with gender stereotypical understanding of sexual

---

[416] WHO, *INSPIRE—Seven Strategies for Ending Violence against Children*, Geneva 2016, p. 16.

[417] UNICEF, *Research on the Sexual Exploitation of Boys: Findings, ethical considerations and methodological challenges*, p. 6; citing a Norwegian study which concluded that the strongest predictor of accepting attitudes towards child sexual abuse was views supporting male power towards women, UNICEF, *Action to End Child Sexual Exploitation and Abuse. A Review of the Evidence*, New York 2020, p. 48; ACERWC, *General Comment No. 7 on Art 27 of the African Charter on the Rights and Welfare of the Child*, paras. 35, 113.

[418] CRC Committee, *Guidelines regarding the implementation of the Optional Protocol to the Convention on the Rights of the Child on the sale of children, child prostitution and child pornography*, CRC/C/156, para. 33; as mentioned before, it is unfortunate that despite acknowledging the vulnerability of 'children of other gender or sex identities' in para. 13 of the Guidelines, they only speak about boys and girls when requiring a gender-specific perspective.

[419] Raewyn Connell, *Masculinities*, Berkeley 1995, p. 83.

[420] ACERWC, *General Comment No. 7 on Art 27 of the African Charter on the Rights and Welfare of the Child*, para. 8; American Psychological Association, *Early socialization of negative masculine ideals*, September 2018, available here: https://www.apa.org/pi/about/newsletter/2018/09/harmful-masculinity (last accessed: 12 December 2021).

violence.[421] Such laws reproduce patriarchal structures and narratives and therefore hamper the combatting of root causes of violence against children.

In line with the socio-ecological model, vulnerabilities on a societal level such as the gender vulnerabilities described above further interact with vulnerabilities on individual level (e.g. sex, age, education, income, sexual orientation), close-relationship level (e.g. poor parenting practices, family dysfunction, children witnessing violence against mother or step mother) and community level (e.g. poverty, high population density, low social cohesion, high crime rates).[422] Therefore, States parties should employ prevention strategies which address the various levels of vulnerability in a holistic and interrelated manner. A model for such a comprehensive, child-centred prevention approach is the INSPIRE strategy, which includes seven strategies which together provide an overarching framework for ending violence against children.[423] The CRC Committee for example recommends providing social protection support and economic empowerment programmes for vulnerable families to be employed in conjunction with preventing harmful practices and mandatory screening of all personnel working with children.[424] Considering that the levels described in the socio-ecological model vary from country to country, any measure for the prevention of OPSC offences should be evidence based.

Further, the CRC Committee clearly requires States parties to take measures targeting the demand for children for the purpose of committing OPSC offences.[425] A concrete example of such a measure is the provision of intervention and assistance measures for people with a sexual interest in children or who consider themselves at risk of committing an OPSC offence. The term 'paedophile', i.e. a person with a primarily sexual interest in prepubescent children, is often (and wrongly) interchangeably used with 'child sex offender': not every person sexually abusing children is a 'paedophile', and not every 'paedophile' is a child sex

---

[421] ACERWC, *General Comment No. 7 on Art 27 of the African Charter on the Rights and Welfare of the Child*, para. 15.

[422] WHO, *INSPIRE—Seven Strategies for Ending Violence against Children*, Geneva 2016, p. 16.

[423] Ibid., pp. 28 et seq.

[424] CRC Committee, *Guidelines regarding the implementation of the Optional Protocol to the Convention on the Rights of the Child on the sale of children, child prostitution and child pornography*, CRC/C/156, para. 33–34; with a differentiated view on the creation of sex offender registries, see ECPAT, *Explanatory Report to the Guidelines Regarding the Implementation of the Optional Protocol to the Convention on the Rights of the Child on the Sale of Children, Child Prostitution and Child Pornography*, p. 47.

[425] CRC Committee, *Guidelines regarding the implementation of the Optional Protocol to the Convention on the Rights of the Child on the sale of children, child prostitution and child pornography*, CRC/C/156, para. 32.

offender.[426] However, the demonisation of the term 'paedophile' makes it diffi-cult for people to seek help and for receiving the necessary services so they do not become offenders.[427] Considering the stigma attached to 'paedophiles', inter-ventions should guarantee the right to privacy and, where possible, guarantee anonymity.[428] Online and telephonic reporting services are therefore particularly suitable to create an open space for people who are at risk of offending to seek help.[429]

The CRC Committee further recommends specific measures for preventing OPSC offences in the context of travel and tourism and where these offences are committed online. For SECTT, the Committee recommends the adoption and enforcement of corporate polices and strategies to prevent sexual exploitation.[430] Further, the private sector should make use of technologies to track and block payments for OPSC offences in the context of travel and tourism.[431] States Parties should also employ measures to ensure convicted offenders are not reoffending, for example by putting in place travel restrictions for convicted offenders and through improved cross-border exchange of information.[432]

With regard to online facilitated offences, States parties should work closely with the private sector to develop adequate prevention strategies.[433] Considering that child sexual abuse material shared on the internet perpetuates the trauma of

---

[426] Persons accessing child sexual abuse material often might be drawn to these images due to a desensitization through consumption of extreme adult pornography not because of a primary sex-ual interest in children, WeProtect Global Alliance, *Global Threat Assessment 2021*, p. 45; see reports from Lucy Faithfull Foundation stating that only 15–20% of the offenders they work with are consid-ered 'pedophiles', see WeProtect Global Alliance, *Global Threat Assessment 2021*, p. 6; see also ECPAT, *Terminology Guidelines for the Protection of Children from Sexual Exploitation and Sexual Abuse*, p. 84.

[427] BBC News, *'Paedophiles need help, not condemnation—I should know'*, 10 February 2017, avail-able here: https://www.bbc.co.uk/bbcthree/article/3216b48d-3195-4f67-8149-54586689ae3c (last accessed: 12 December 2021).

[428] ECPAT, *Explanatory Report to the Guidelines Regarding the Implementation of the Optional Protocol to the Convention on the Rights of the Child on the Sale of Children, Child Prostitution and Child Pornography*, p. 45.

[429] As an example, the UK-based Lucy Faithfull Foundation collaborated with the adult pornog-raphy website Pornhub to place deterrence messages for people searching for child sexual abuse material on Pornhub, and referring them to an online self-directed intervention, see WeProtect Global Alliance, *Global Threat Assessment 2021*, p. 46; ECPAT, *Explanatory Report to the Guidelines Regarding the Implementation of the Optional Protocol to the Convention on the Rights of the Child on the Sale of Children, Child Prostitution and Child Pornography*, p. 45.

[430] CRC Committee, *Guidelines regarding the implementation of the Optional Protocol to the Convention on the Rights of the Child on the sale of children, child prostitution and child pornography*, CRC/C/156, para. 36.

[431] Ibid.

[432] Ibid.

[433] Ibid., para. 38; an example of the formulation of a response framework for digital service pro-viders, see Leiden Universiteit/Waag, *Code for Children's Rights*, Leiden 2021.

child survivors, States parties are requested to work with internet service providers to block and remove such content as part of their prevention measures.[434] Technological tools such as 'hashing' and 'hash-matching' are key to detect and identify known child sexual abuse material.[435] Further, the development of technologies such as content classifiers should be prioritised to train AI to identify and categorise new child sexual abuse material.[436] Child sexual abuse material used in criminal trials as evidence should be destroyed after the trial has been concluded.[437] When establishing age verification systems to prevent children from being exposed to content or contact harm, data protection and safeguarding requirements need to be upheld.[438]

Lastly, the CRC Committee states that 'the investigation and prosecution of offenders can also serve as a means of [...] prevention of other similar offences through deterrence'. This statement needs to be read with some caution. Firstly, investigation and prosecution alone are unlikely to have a deterrent effect, as this will be mainly attributed to successful convictions. Secondly, it is important to note that a deterrent effect is largely attributed to the *certainty* of punishment, rather than the *severity* of punishment. This means that knowing that punishment is likely or certain has a more of a deterrent effect than simply imposing high sentences.[439] Therefore, increasing the sentence for a specific offence or setting a mandatory minimum sentence is often more of a political gesture, as it is

---

[434] CRC Committee, *Guidelines regarding the implementation of the Optional Protocol to the Convention on the Rights of the Child on the sale of children, child prostitution and child pornography*, CRC/C/156, paras. 41, 103; although the removal of child sexual abuse material should be a priority for law enforcement, even resource rich countries such as Germany struggle with this, citing limited resources within police, see (in German) NDR, *Kindesmissbrauch: Warum löscht die Polizei die Bilder nicht?*, 2 December 2021, available here: https://daserste.ndr.de/panorama/archiv/2021/Kindesmissbrauch-Warum-loescht-die-Polizei-die-Bilder-nicht,kindesmissbrauch396.html (last accessed: 2 October 2022).

[435] WeProtect Global Alliance, *Global Threat Assessment 2021*, p. 53; stressing the need for international cooperation to increase the number of hashes, ACERWC, *General Comment No. 7 on Art 27 of the African Charter on the Rights and Welfare of the Child*, para. 100.

[436] Ibid.

[437] CRC Committee, *Guidelines regarding the implementation of the Optional Protocol to the Convention on the Rights of the Child on the sale of children, child prostitution and child pornography*, CRC/C/156, para. 76.

[438] CRC Committee, *General comment No. 25 (2021) on children's rights in relation to the digital environment*, CRC/C/GC/25, para. 114.

[439] Valerie Wright, *Deterrence in Criminal Justice—Evaluating Certainty vs. Severity of Punishment*, Washington 2010, available here: https://www.sentencingproject.org/wp-content/uploads/2016/01/Deterrence-in-Criminal-Justice.pdf (last accessed: 12 December 2021).

much easier than addressing the root causes and drivers of such offences (see also section 3.2.3.3).[440]

3.2.9.2 Art 9 (2): Awareness Raising and Training

> 2. States Parties shall promote awareness in the public at large, including children, through information by all appropriate means, education and training, about the preventive measures and harmful effects of the offences referred to in the present Protocol. In fulfilling their obligations under this Article, States Parties shall encourage the participation of the community and, in particular, children and child victims, in such information and education and training programmes, including at the international level.

Art 9 (2) mandates States parties to promote information, education and training on preventive measures and the harmful effects of OPSC offences to the public at large, including children. Judging from the wording, the state obligation seems to be limited as it does not require states to provide for dedicated and specialised training courses for persons working with children and limits the content of any awareness raising campaign to the preventive measures and harmful effects of OPSC.[441]

However, this narrow interpretation of the wording of Art 9 (2) has been considerably expanded in the OPSC Guidelines. The CRC Committee requires States parties to disseminate information about the OPSC to government officials at all levels, all professional persons who have regular contact with children, and the public at large including families and children. For the latter, information needs to be presented in a child-friendly and child-sensitive manner. To build resilience amongst children, they should receive comprehensive sexuality education, including appropriate materials on the sale and sexual exploitation of children both online and offline.[442] Recent research studies have further shown that the myth of 'stranger danger' cannot be substantiated for online offences against children, as has already long been proven inaccurate for offline offences. This needs to influence the design of awareness raising campaigns, which often still

---

[440] For an in-depth discussion on the rationale and constitutionality of minimum mandatory sentences for sexual offences in South Africa, see Baehr, *Mandatory minimum making minimal difference: Ten years of sentencing sex offenders in South Africa.*

[441] Tobin, *The Optional Protocol on the Sale of Children, Child Prostitution, and Child Pornography*, p. 1775.

[442] CRC Committee, *Guidelines regarding the implementation of the Optional Protocol to the Convention on the Rights of the Child on the sale of children, child prostitution and child pornography*, CRC/C/156, para. 28.

conceptualised based on this outdated myth.[443] Lastly, all persons, especially those caring for children, shall be capacitated to detect and report any suspected cases of the sale and sexual exploitation of children. Parents, caregivers and teachers play a crucial role in helping children to realise their rights in the digital environment and therefore require dedicated digital literacy training.[444] In this context, parents and caregivers should also be sensitised towards respecting the child's right to privacy, ensuring that the level of monitoring is proportionate and respects the child's evolving capacity.[445]

In addition, online literacy training is key for building children's digital resilience and should be taught as part of the basic curriculum from preschool level onwards.[446] These courses should cover the safe application of digital tools and resources, fact checking of online sources and identification of misinformation, identification and impact of exposure to risks relating to content, contact, conduct and contract and coping strategies to reduce harm.[447] As a consequence, it is obviously necessary to capacitate teachers to teach all the above subjects, especially teachers involved in digital literacy education and sexual and reproductive health education.[448] Considering the increased vulnerability of children outside the school system, educational training should be extended to children outside the formal schools system. Lastly, the media should be capacitated on issues

---

[443] Showing that in most cases the perpetrator is known to the child, ECPAT/INTERPOL/ UNICEF, *Disrupting harm in Kenya: Evidence on online child sexual exploitation and abuse*, Bangkok/ Lyon/Florence 2021, p. 93; ECPAT/INTERPOL/UNICEF, *Disrupting harm in Uganda: Evidence on online child sexual exploitation and abuse*, Bangkok/Lyon/Florence 2021, p. 97; ECPAT/INTERPOL/ UNICEF, *Disrupting harm in Thailand: Evidence on online child sexual exploitation and abuse*, Bangkok/Lyon/Florence 2022, p. 97; ECPAT/INTERPOL/UNICEF, *Disrupting harm in Tanzania: Evidence on online child sexual exploitation and abuse*, Bangkok/Lyon/Florence 2022, p. 88; ECPAT/ INTERPOL/UNICEF, *Disrupting harm in Ethiopia: Evidence on online child sexual exploitation and abuse*, Bangkok/Lyon/Florence 2022, p. 44; the only exception amongst the available *Disrupting Harm* studies are the Philippines, showing that in most cases the online sexual abuse and exploitation is committed by a perpetrator unknown to the child, see ECPAT/INTERPOL/UNICEF, *Disrupting harm in the Philippines: Evidence on online child sexual exploitation and abuse*, Bangkok/ Lyon/Florence 2022.

[444] CRC Committee, *General comment No. 25 (2021) on children's rights in relation to the digital environment*, CRC/C/GC/25, paras. 21, 105.

[445] Ibid., para. 76.

[446] Ibid., para. 104; Cliff Manning, *A framework for digital resilience: supporting children through an enabling environment*, LSE Blog, 20 January 2021, available here: https://blogs.lse.ac.uk/parenting 4digitalfuture/2021/01/20/digital-resilience/ (last accessed: 12 December 2021).

[447] CRC Committee, *General comment No. 25 (2021) on children's rights in relation to the digital environment*, CRC/C/GC/25, para. 104.

[448] Ibid.

pertaining to OPSC offences, with a particular focus on correct terminology and protection of the identity and privacy of affected children.[449]

3.2.9.3 Art 9 (3): Reintegration and Recovery

> 3. States Parties shall take all feasible measures with the aim of ensuring all appropri-
> ate assistance to victims of such offences, including their full social reintegration and
> their full physical and psychological recovery.

Building on the obligation stipulated in Art 39 CRC, the OPSC requires states to take all 'feasible measures' to assist child survivors of OPSC offences in their reintegration and recovery process. This formulation seems to stand in contrast to the more comprehensive obligation of States parties to take all 'appropriate measures' under Art 39 CRC.[450] Such a restrictive interpretation does not seem to be aligned with the reading of the CRC Committee which provides for clear measures to fulfil States parties' obligation towards reintegration and recovery of child survivors in the OPSC Guidelines. It requires the availability of medical, physical and psychological recovery and social integration services, with trained and certified personnel providing such services to children countrywide and free of charge.[451] Further, the CRC Committee requires the provision of a continuum of care, including post-trial reintegration services to all survivors, including for non-citizens of the relevant state.[452] In the case of separated children, family reunification plays an important role in the recovery of the child survivor. Considering that the family environment might remain unsafe for some children, alternative measures need to be discussed with the child in line with CRC General Comment No. 21. Institutionalised care should be a measure of last resort, with preference being given to providing care to the survivor in family-type settings.[453]

Specific attention needs to be paid to the complexities concerning the recovery of online child sexual abuse survivors. As has been alluded to before, the constant threat of the abuse imagery re-surfacing on the Internet and other people

---

[449] CRC Committee, *Guidelines regarding the implementation of the Optional Protocol to the Convention on the Rights of the Child on the sale of children, child prostitution and child pornography*, CRC/C/156, para. 28.

[450] Tobin, *The Optional Protocol on the Sale of Children, Child Prostitution, and Child Pornography*, p. 1776.

[451] CRC Committee, *Guidelines regarding the implementation of the Optional Protocol to the Convention on the Rights of the Child on the sale of children, child prostitution and child pornography*, CRC/C/156, para. 100.

[452] Ibid.

[453] ECPAT, *Explanatory Report to the Guidelines Regarding the Implementation of the Optional Protocol to the Convention on the Rights of the Child on the Sale of Children, Child Prostitution and Child Pornography*, p. 96.

accessing it makes it often impossible for survivors to close the chapter and focus on their recovery. The CRC Committee recommends that 'States parties should increase awareness about such situations and take adequate measures to provide long-term social and psychological services as needed'.[454] The possibility of continued circulation of such materials also exacerbates the child's stigmatization and the same victimization the child and their family might feel. Therefore, the CRC Committee stresses the importance of 'blocking and removing harmful material involving children'.[455] An additional layer of complexity is added for situations where law enforcement discovers child sexual abuse material on the internet but does not know whether the victim is aware that their abuse has been documented and shared online. Informing the survivor could cause additional distress and throw the victim back in their recovery process. At the same time, it could be argued that a survivor has the right to know this information to give them the opportunity to re-establish agency and create ownership.[456] States parties therefore need to find survivor-centred solutions to these complexities in the recovery process while putting the best interests of the child first.

3.2.9.4 Art 9 (4): Compensation for Damages

> 4. States Parties shall ensure that all child victims of the offences described in the present Protocol have access to adequate procedures to seek, without discrimination, compensation for damages from those legally responsible.

According to Art 9 (4), States parties shall ensure that child survivors of OPSC offences have access to adequate compensation from those legally responsible. The term 'shall' points towards a strict state obligation in this area. The CRC Committee in its Guidelines has further specified the actions States parties need to undertake to provide adequate compensation to survivors. Firstly, the CRC Committee states that various forms of compensation, not only financial payments, need to be available to the survivor. To decide which form of compensation is most suitable for a child survivor, their specific situation, personal opinion and prospects for life should be taken into consideration. As an alternative or

---

[454] CRC Committee, *Guidelines regarding the implementation of the Optional Protocol to the Convention on the Rights of the Child on the sale of children, child prostitution and child pornography*, CRC/C/156, para. 102.

[455] Ibid., para. 103.

[456] Suzanne Ost/Alisdair A. Gillespie, *To know or not to know: should crimes regarding photographs of their child sexual abuse be disclosed to now-adult, unknowing victims?*, International Review of Victimology, Vol. 25 (2018).

addendum to financial compensation, support could be provided for educational or income-generating activities.[457]

There are various avenues available as to how the child can seek compensation, depending on the national legal system. Some countries integrate compensation claims into their criminal proceedings, others require children to file a separate lawsuit at the civil courts. Another option is to seek compensation from state managed victim compensation funds.[458] Across all avenues, children face considerable challenges in accessing compensation. Children might lack legal representation, or they are not made aware of the compensation schemes available to them; state compensation funds might not be tailored towards child victims and they are often intertwined with the criminal justice process; the complexity of transnational cases might create barriers to access compensation.[459] In order to mitigate these challenges, the CRC Committee makes it clear that children should be supported in their efforts to seek compensation, for example through providing free legal aid.[460] States further need to ensure that children are not considered ineligible for compensation schemes if they were involved in the offences in question. Lastly, if children can only seek compensation through civil courts, the same child-friendly and gender-sensitive measures discussed under Art 8 in the context of criminal procedures should be applied to the civil procedures.[461] States should further take action to ensure that money laundering laws enable child survivors to get paid from forfeited assets.[462]

The above challenges are further complicated in online child sexual abuse and exploitation cases. Children suffer multi-dimensional harm in these offences, which is often difficult to calculate.[463] Physical and psychological harm, including costs for counselling or loss of earnings due to the victim's inability to work, and the continuous violation of the victim's privacy and dignity are not easily quantifiable. However, the financial compensation, especially when it comes directly from

---

[457] CRC Committee, *Guidelines regarding the implementation of the Optional Protocol to the Convention on the Rights of the Child on the sale of children, child prostitution and child pornography*, CRC/C/156, para. 100.

[458] ECPAT, *Barriers to Compensation for Child Victims of Sexual Exploitation*, Bangkok 2017, pp. 15 et seq.; UN Economic and Social Council, *Guidelines on Justice in Matters involving Child Victims and Witnesses of Crime*, E/CN.15/2005/L.2/Ref.1, para. 37.

[459] ECPAT, *Barriers to Compensation for Child Victims of Sexual Exploitation*, pp. 22 et seq.

[460] CRC Committee, *Guidelines regarding the implementation of the Optional Protocol to the Convention on the Rights of the Child on the sale of children, child prostitution and child pornography*, CRC/C/156, para. 97.

[461] Ibid., para. 104.

[462] Ibid., para. 106.

[463] Ibid., para. 105.

the perpetrator, is an important aspect in the reparation paid to the victim.[464] Besides the financial reparation, additional measures need to be put in place to assist the victim's restoration, such as specialised counselling by trained personnel who understand the complex trauma survivors of online child sexual abuse experience.[465]

3.2.9.5 Art 9 (5): Prohibition of Advertising OPSC Offences

> 5. States Parties shall take appropriate measures aimed at effectively prohibiting the production and dissemination of material advertising the offences described in the present Protocol.

Art 9 (5) obliges States parties to take all appropriate measures to curb the production and dissemination of material advertising OPSC offences. Even though the wording of the provisions does not specify which exact measures need to be taken as long as they are effective, the CRC Committee in its Guidelines stipulates that the publication of material advertising or promoting the sexual exploitation of children should be criminalised.[466] Criminal law is therefore recommended as most suitable regulatory measure to effectively prohibit the advertisement of OPSC offences.

3.2.10 *Art 10 OPSC: International Cooperation*

3.2.10.1 Art 10 (1): Cooperation to Strengthen Transnational Law Enforcement Collaboration

> 1. States Parties shall take all necessary steps to strengthen international cooperation by multilateral, regional and bilateral arrangements for the prevention, detection, investigation, prosecution and punishment of those responsible for acts involving the sale of children, child prostitution, child pornography and child sex tourism. States Parties shall also promote international cooperation and coordination between their authorities, national and international non-governmental organizations and international organizations.

Art 10 (1) sets out the states' obligation to take all necessary steps to strengthen international collaboration in the area of law enforcement, using multilateral, regional and bilateral mechanisms, hereby complementing and reinforcing Art 34 and 35 CRC and Arts 4–7. As mentioned before, Art 10 is the only provision in the

---

[464] Suzanne Ost, *A new paradigm of reparation for victims of child pornography*, Legal Studies, Vol. 36 (2016), p. 620.

[465] Ibid., p. 637.

[466] CRC Committee, *Guidelines regarding the implementation of the Optional Protocol to the Convention on the Rights of the Child on the sale of children, child prostitution and child pornography*, CRC/C/156, para. 66.

OPSC which makes explicit reference to 'child sex tourism'. A possible explanation for this is that child sexual abuse and exploitation in travel and tourism typically have a transnational element and hence require strong international cooperation mechanisms to prevent and respond to such offences. Close international cooperation is further crucial in online child sexual abuse and exploitation cases due to the cross-border and transnational nature of the digital environment.[467] Such collaboration should cover 'effective detection and reporting systems, information-sharing, and safeguarding and transmission of evidence of crimes, including electronic evidence, in a timely manner'.[468] In addition, victim identification should form part of international cooperation efforts, including aspects of rescue and repatriation.[469] States parties should strengthen collaboration with international and national NGOs and organizations, as well as the private sector 'to develop the technological tools necessary to enable the identification, investigation and prosecution of offenders before the courts, as well as identification of victims'.[470] The private sector should further comply with law enforcement measures to facilitate access to evidence relevant for the investigation of OPSC offences.[471]

3.2.10.2 Art 10 (2): Cooperation to Strengthen Recovery, Reintegration and Repatriation

> 2. States Parties shall promote international cooperation to assist child victims in their physical and psychological recovery, social reintegration and repatriation.

Art 10 (2) expands the scope of the State party obligation set out in Art 9 (3) to assist child survivors of OPSC offences in their recovery and reintegration. In contrast to Art 10 (1), the States parties shall merely 'promote' international cooperation to assist child survivors in their recovery, reintegration and repatriation. Neither the OPSC nor the OPSC Guidelines provide for clear guidance on how such international cooperation should be promoted. In an earlier draft of the OPSC, the timely

---

[467] CRC Committee, *General comment No. 25 (2021) on children's rights in relation to the digital environment*, CRC/C/GC/25, para. 123.

[468] Ibid., para. 124; UN Economic and Social Council, *Guidelines on Justice in Matters involving Child Victims and Witnesses of Crime*, E/CN.15/2005/L.2/Ref.1, para. 44; CRC Committee, *Guidelines regarding the implementation of the Optional Protocol to the Convention on the Rights of the Child on the sale of children, child prostitution and child pornography*, CRC/C/156, para. 109.

[469] CRC Committee, *Guidelines regarding the implementation of the Optional Protocol to the Convention on the Rights of the Child on the sale of children, child prostitution and child pornography*, CRC/C/156, para. 101.

[470] Ibid., para. 111.

[471] Ibid., para. 112.

repatriation of child survivors was mentioned as one concrete measure. However, this formulation was dropped later on.[472]

3.2.10.3 Art 10 (3): Cooperation to Strengthen Prevention

> 3. States Parties shall promote the strengthening of international cooperation in order to address the root causes, such as poverty and underdevelopment, contributing to the vulnerability of children to the sale of children, child prostitution, child pornography and child sex tourism.

Art 10 (3) expands the States parties obligation set out under Art 9 (1) for taking preventative measures to the international stage. According to Art 10 (3), States parties shall promote the strengthening international cooperation to address the root causes and contributing factors for OPSC offences. Considering the increased globalization and digitalization of the world, root causes and drivers span across country borders and hence require a coordinated response. Unfortunately, neither the OPSC nor the OPSC guidelines provide for concrete examples of which measures should be undertaken to fulfil the obligation under Art 10 (3).

3.2.10.4 Art 10 (4): Obligation to Provide Support to Other States

> 4. States Parties in a position to do so shall provide financial, technical or other assistance through existing multilateral, regional, bilateral or other programmes.

Art 10 (4) complements the more specific provisions under Art 10 (1)–(3) for increased international cooperation by asking States parties 'in a position to do so' to provide financial, technical or any other support through existing international, regional, bilateral or other programmes. This could include support for development programmes, poverty eradication and universal education.[473] The formulation 'States parties in a position to do so' is not further specified and hence leaves considerable room for interpretation. Even though this weakens the legal force of this provision, it at least offers States parties in need of support an entry point to request assistance from financially stronger states.[474]

---

[472] Tobin, *The Optional Protocol on the Sale of Children, Child Prostitution, and Child Pornography*, p. 1781.

[473] CRC Committee, *Guidelines regarding the implementation of the Optional Protocol to the Convention on the Rights of the Child on the sale of children, child prostitution and child pornography*, CRC/C/156, para. 110.

[474] Tobin, *The Optional Protocol on the Sale of Children, Child Prostitution, and Child Pornography*, p. 1782.

3.2.11 *Art 11 OPSC: Conflict of Norms*

Nothing in the present Protocol shall affect any provisions that are more conducive to the realization of the rights of the child and that may be contained in:
(a) The law of a State Party;
(b) International law in force for that State.

Art 11 is the pendant to Art 41 CRC and stipulates that in case national law or international law to which the state is a party, sets a higher standard for the realisation of children's rights, then this standard should prevail.

3.2.12 *Art 12 OPSC: Reporting Obligations*

1. Each State Party shall, within two years following the entry into force of the present Protocol for that State Party, submit a report to the Committee on the Rights of the Child providing comprehensive information on the measures it has taken to implement the provisions of the Protocol.
2. Following the submission of the comprehensive report, each State Party shall include in the reports they submit to the Committee on the Rights of the Child, in accordance with article 44 of the Convention, any further information with respect to the implementation of the present Protocol. Other States Parties to the Protocol shall submit a report every five years.
3. The Committee on the Rights of the Child may request from States Parties further information relevant to the implementation of the present Protocol.

Art 12 regulates the States parties' reporting obligations and in many ways reflects Art 44 CRC. Art 12 (1) sets out that the first state party report is due two years after the entry into force of the OPSC for the state party. From there, updates on the implementation of the OPSC should be included in the CRC state party reports which are due every 5 years (Art 44 (1) CRC). If a OPSC state party is not a state party to the CRC, then stand-alone OPSC reports are due every 5 years, see Art 12 (2).[475] The CRC Committee may further request additional information from the state party according to Art 12 (3). To ensure that high quality reports are submitted in a timely fashion, the CRC Committee issued several guidelines on the state party reporting.[476]

It is important to note that the CRC Committee enacted a simplified reporting procedure effective 1 September 2019.[477] The Committee sends to the State party

---

[475] At the moment, the US is the only country which is a State party to the OPSC but not to the CRC and hence submits regular reports in line with Art 12 (2).

[476] For more information on the various reporting guidelines, see here: https://www.ohchr.org /en/treaty-bodies/crc/reporting-guidelines (last accessed: 24 April 2022).

[477] For more information on the simplified reporting mechanism, see ibid.

that accepted the simplified reporting procedure a request for specific information (List of Issues Prior to Reporting, hereafter: LOIPR). The State party's replies to the questions constitute the State party's report to the Committee. Differently from the standard reporting procedure, the States parties are no longer required to submit to the Committee both a State party report and written replies to a list of issues. This aims to promote and incentivise timely and quality submissions from States parties. However, the simplified reporting procedure also carries the risk that State party reports are limited, as the LOIPR prepared by the Committee might not cover all relevant topics which are present in the respective reporting country. This could ultimately hamper the accountability of States parties for their obligations under the CRC and OPSC.

3.2.13 *Art 13 OPSC: Signature, Ratification and Accession*

1. The present Protocol is open for signature by any State that is a party to the Convention or has signed it.
2. The present Protocol is subject to ratification and is open to accession by any State that is a party to the Convention or has signed it. Instruments of ratification or accession shall be deposited with the Secretary- General of the United Nations.

Art 13 (1) stipulates state the OPSC is open for signature by any state that is a party to the Convention on the Rights of the Child or has signed it. As set out in section 3.1.1, this provision considerably threatened the final adoption of the OPSC text during the drafting process. The main question was whether states that did not ratify the CRC could become States parties to the OPSC. The current regulation requiring States parties who intend to sign the OPSC must have at least signed (not ratified) the CRC, is a compromise which States parties could agree upon in the drafting process. Same applies *mutatis mutandis* for states who intend to ratify the OPSC. Lastly, Art 13 (2) states that instruments of ratification or accession need to be deposited with the Secretary General of the United Nations.

3.2.14 *Art 14 OPSC: Entry into Force*

1. The present Protocol shall enter into force three months after the deposit of the tenth instrument of ratification or accession.
2. For each State ratifying the present Protocol or acceding to it after its entry into force, the Protocol shall enter into force one month after the date of the deposit of its own instrument of ratification or accession.

Art 14 (1) sets out that the OPSC enters into force three months after the deposit of the tenth instrument of ratification or accession. This requirement was satisfied

on the 18 January 2002.[478] According to Art 14 (2), for every state which ratifies or accedes to the OPSC after its entry into force, the OPSC will enter into force one month after the date of the deposit.

3.2.15 Art 15 OPSC: Denunciation

1. Any State Party may denounce the present Protocol at any time by written notification to the Secretary- General of the United Nations, who shall thereafter inform the other States Parties to the Convention and all States that have signed the Convention. The denunciation shall take effect one year after the date of receipt of the notification by the Secretary-General.
2. Such a denunciation shall not have the effect of releasing the State Party from its obligations under the present Protocol in regard to any offence that occurs prior to the date on which the denunciation becomes effective. Nor shall such a denunciation prejudice in any way the continued consideration of any matter that is already under consideration by the Committee on the Rights of the Child prior to the date on which the denunciation becomes effective.

Similar to Art 50 CRC, Art 15 (1) States parties may denounce the OPSC at any time by written notification to the Secretary General of the United Nations, who then needs to inform the States parties and signatories of the OPSC. The denunciation then takes effect one year after the Secretary General was notified.

However, Art 15 (2) makes it clear that following the denunciation, the state party is still bound by the OPSC until the date the denunciation becomes effective. In the same vein, any pending matters at the CRC Committee concerning the denouncing state shall not be prejudiced up until the date on which the denunciation becomes effective.

3.2.16 Art 16 OPSC: Amendment

1. Any State Party may propose an amendment and file it with the Secretary-General of the United Nations. The Secretary-General shall thereupon communicate the proposed amendment to States Parties with a request that they indicate whether they favour a conference of States Parties for the purpose of considering and voting upon the proposals. If, within four months from the date of such communication, at least one third of the States Parties favour such a conference, the Secretary-General shall convene the conference under the auspices of the United Nations. Any amendment

---

[478] Tobin, *The Optional Protocol on the Sale of Children, Child Prostitution, and Child Pornography,* p. 1784.

adopted by a majority of States Parties present and voting at the conference shall be submitted to the General Assembly of the United Nations for approval.

2. An amendment adopted in accordance with paragraph 1 of the present article shall enter into force when it has been approved by the General Assembly and accepted by a two-thirds majority of States Parties.

3. When an amendment enters into force, it shall be binding on those States Parties that have accepted it, other States Parties still being bound by the provisions of the present Protocol and any earlier amendments they have accepted.

Art 16 sets out the detailed procedure for amendment of the OPSC. It is identical with Art 50 CRC. The text of Art 16 is self-explanatory, and no additional comments will therefore be submitted.[479]

3.2.17 *Art 17 OPSC: Languages*

1. The present Protocol, of which the Arabic, Chinese, English, French, Russian and Spanish texts are equally authentic, shall be deposited in the archives of the United Nations.

2. The Secretary-General of the United Nations shall transmit certified copies of the present Protocol to all States Parties to the Convention and all States that have signed the Convention.

Art 17 (1) requires that the OPSC, of which the Arabic, Chinese, English, French, Russian, and Spanish texts are equally authentic, be deposited in the archives of the United Nations. This stands in contrast to the CRC, for which Art 54 CRC requires that the Convention is deposited with the Secretary General of the United Nations. Art 17 (2) mandates the Secretary General of the United Nations to transmit certified copies of the OPSC to all States parties and signatories of the OPSC.

---

[479] As a note, there was only one CRC amendment which was adopted on 12 December 1995 and which increased the number of experts on the CRC Committee from 10 to 18 experts, see here: https://treaties.un.org/doc/Treaties/1998/05/19980501%2004-05%20AM/Ch_IV_11_ap.pdf (last accessed: 24 April 2022).

CHAPTER FOUR

OPSC IN CONTINUOUS NEED OF REVIEW IN A GLOBALISED, DIGITALISED AND RAPIDLY CHANGING WORLD

The above analysis of the OPSC demonstrates the impact of globalisation, digitalisation and COVID-19 on the vulnerabilities of children towards sale and sexual exploitation, and clearly identifies the important role of the OPSC Guidelines and CRC Commentary No. 25 to ensure the OPSC remains relevant and effective against the emerging forms of sale and sexual exploitation of children.

At the same time, it is important to acknowledge that due to the fast pace at which the digital and globalised world develops, the recommendations in the Guidelines and General Comment No. 25 might be outdated soon. Therefore, the CRC Committee is required to continuously update and develop its jurisprudence on the issue to ensure its recommendations speak to the reality on the ground.[480]

---

[480] Ann Skelton/Benyam Mezmur, *Technology changing @ a Dizzying Pace: Reflections on Selected Jurisprudence of the UN Committee on the Rights of the Child and Technology*, Peace Human Rights Governance, Vol. 3 (2019), p. 296.

BIBLIOGRAPHY

ACERWC, *General Comment No. 7 on Art 27 of the African Charter on the Rights and Welfare of the Child*, Maseru 2021.

African Union Commission, *Joint general comment of the African Commission on Human and People's Rights and the African Committee of Experts on the Rights and Welfare of the Child on ending child marriages*, Addis Ababa 2017.

American Psychological Association, *Early socialization of negative masculine ideals*, September 2018, available here: https://www.apa.org/pi/about/newsletter/2018/09/harmful-masculinity (last accessed: 12 December 2021).

BBC, *Larry Nassar case: The 156 women who confronted a predator*, 25 January 2018, available here: https://www.bbc.com/news/world-us-canada-42725339 (last accessed: 14 June 2022).

BBC News, *'Paedophiles need help, not condemnation—I should know'*, 10 February 2017, available here: https://www.bbc.co.uk/bbcthree/article/3216b48d-3195-4f67-8149-5458 6689ae3c (last accessed: 12 December 2021).

BBC News, *Simone Biles: 'I blame system that enabled Larry Nassar abuse'*, 15 September 2021, available here: https://www.bbc.com/news/world-us-canada-58573887 (last accessed: 2 October 2021).

Brenner, Susan W./Koops, Bert-Jaap, *Approaches to Cybercrime Jurisdiction*, Journal of High Technology Law, Vol. 4 (2004).

Carpenter, Belinda et al., *Harm, Responsibility, Age, and Consent*, New Criminal Law Review: An International and Interdisciplinary Journal, Vol. 17 (2014).

CEDAW Committee/CRC Committee, *Joint general recommendation/general comment No. 31 of the Committee on the Elimination of Discrimination against Women and No. 18 of the Committee on the Rights of the Child on harmful practices*, CEDAW/C/GC31-CRC/C/GC/18 (4 November 2014).

CEDAW Committee/CRC Committee, *Joint general recommendation/general comment No. 31 of the Committee on the Elimination of Discrimination against Women and No. 18 of the Committee on the Rights of the Child (2019) on harmful practices*, CEDAW/C/GC31/Rev.1-CRC/C/GC/18/Rev.1 (8 May 2019).

Center for Reproductive Rights, *Submission from the Center for Reproductive Rights following the call for inputs by the Special Rapporteur on the Sale and Sexual Exploitation of Children on Safeguards for the protection of the rights of children born from surrogate arrangements*, New York (undated).

Commission on Human Rights, *Sale of Children*, E/CN.4/RES/1990/68.

Connell, Raewyn, *Masculinities*, Berkeley 1995.

CRC Committee, *Concluding observations on the report submitted by Czechia under article 12 (1) of the Optional Protocol to the Convention on the Rights of the Child on the sale of children, child prostitution and child pornography*, CRC/C/OPSC/CZE/CO/1 (5 March 2019).

CRC Committee, *Concluding observations on the report submitted by Angola under article 12 (1) of the Optional Protocol to the Convention on the Rights of the Child on the*

sale of children, child prostitution and child pornography, CRC/C/OPSC/AGO/CO/1 (29 June 2018).

CRC Committee, *Concluding observations on the report submitted by Saudi Arabia under article 12 (1) of the Optional Protocol to the Convention on the Rights of the Child on the sale of children, child prostitution and child pornography*, CRC/C/OPSC/SAU/CO/1 (31 October 2018).

CRC Committee, *Concluding observations on the report submitted by South Africa under article 12 (1) of the Optional Protocol to the Convention on the Rights of the Child on the sale of children, child prostitution and child pornography*, CRC/C/OPSC/ZAF/CO/1 (26 October 2016).

CRC Committee, *Concluding observations on the report submitted by Georgia under article 12 (1) of the Optional Protocol to the Convention on the Rights of the Child on the sale of children, child prostitution and child pornography*, CRC/C/OPSC/GEO/CO/1 (30 October 2019).

CRC Committee, *Concluding observations on the report submitted by Tajikistan under article 12 (1) of the Optional Protocol to the Convention on the Rights of the Child on the sale of children, child prostitution and child pornography*, CRC/C/OPSC/TJK/CO/1 (3 November 2017).

CRC Committee, *Concluding observations on the report submitted by Niger under article 12 (1) of the Optional Protocol to the Convention on the Rights of the Child on the sale of children, child prostitution and child pornography*, CRC/C/OPSC/NER/CO/1 (12 December 2018).

CRC Committee, *Concluding observations on the report submitted by Benin under article 12 (1) of the Optional Protocol to the Convention on the Rights of the Child on the sale of children, child prostitution and child pornography*, CRC/C/OPSC/BEN/CO/1 (29 November 2018).

CRC Committee, *Concluding observations on the report submitted by the Russian Federation under article 12 (1) of the Optional Protocol to the Convention on the Rights of the Child on the sale of children, child prostitution and child pornography*, CRC/C/OPSC/RUS/ CO/01.

CRC Committee, *General Comment No. 13: The right of the child to freedom from all forms of violence*, CRC/C/GC/13 (18 April 2011).

CRC Committee, *General comment No. 14 (2013) on the right of the child to have his or her best interests taken as a primary consideration (art. 3, para. 1)*, CRC/C/GC/14 (29 May 2013).

CRC Committee, *General comment No. 16 (2013) on State obligations regarding the impact of the business sector on children's rights*, CRC/C/GC/16 (17 April 2013).

CRC Committee, *General comment No. 25 (2021) on children's rights in relation to the digital environment*, CRC/C/GC/25 (2 March 2021).

CRC Committee, *General Comment No. 4: Adolescent Health and Development in the Context of the Convention on the Rights of the Child*, CRC/GC/2003/04 (1 July 2003).

CRC Committee, *General Comment No. 6 (2005) Treatment of unaccompanied and separated children outside the country of their origin*, CRC/GC/2005/6 (1 September 2005).

CRC Committee, *Guidelines regarding the implementation of the Optional Protocol to the Convention on the Rights of the Child on the sale of children, child prostitution and child pornography*, CRC/C/156 (10 September 2019).

CRC Committee, *Report of the 2014 Day of General Discussion "Digital media and children's rights"*, Geneva 2014, available here: https://www.ohchr.org/Documents/HRBodies /CRC/Discussions/2014/DGD_report.pdf (last accessed: 1 December 2021).

CRC Committee, *Views adopted by the Committee under the Optional Protocol to the Convention on the Rights of the Child on a communications procedure, concerning communication No. 76/2019*, CRC/C/86/D/76/2019 (2021).

de Boer-Buquicchio, Maud, *Report of the special rapporteur on the sale of children, child prostitution and child pornography*, A/71/261 (1 August 2016).

de Boer-Buquicchio, Maud, *Report of the Special Rapporteur on the sale of children, child prostitution and child pornography*, A/HRC/34/55 (22 December 2016).

de Boer-Buquicchio, Maud, *Report of the Special Rapporteur on the sale and sexual exploitation of children, including child prostitution, child pornography and other child sexual abuse material*, A/HRC/37/60 (15 January 2018).

de Boer-Buquicchio, Maud, *Report of the Special Rapporteur on the sale and sexual exploitation of children, including child prostitution, child pornography and other child sexual abuse material*, A/74/162 (15 July 2019).

de Boer-Buquicchio, Maud, *Report of the special rapporteur on the sale and sexual exploitation of children, including child prostitution, child pornography and other child sexual abuse material*, A/HRC/40/51 (27 December 2018), para. 13.

de Boer-Buquicchio, Maud/Grazia Giammarinaro, Maria, *Joint report of the Special Rapporteur on the sale and sexual exploitation of children, including child prostitution, child pornography and other child sexual abuse material and the Special Rapporteur on trafficking in persons, especially women and children*, A/72/164 (18 July 2017).

ECPAT, *Barriers to Compensation for Child Victims of Sexual Exploitation*, Bangkok 2017.

ECPAT, *Explanatory Report to the Guidelines Regarding the Implementation of the Optional Protocol to the Convention on the Rights of the Child on the Sale of Children, Child Prostitution and Child Pornography*, Bangkok 2019.

ECPAT, *Global Study Report on Sexual Exploitation of Children in Travel and Tourism*, Bangkok 2016.

ECPAT, *Terminology Guidelines for the Protection of Children from Sexual Exploitation and Sexual Abuse*, Bangkok 2016.

ECPAT, *Thematic Report: Unrecognized Sexual Abuse and Exploitation of Children in Child, Early and Forced Marriages*, Bangkok 2015.

ECPAT/INTERPOL/UNICEF, *Disrupting harm in Kenya: Evidence on online child sexual exploitation and abuse*, Bangkok/Lyon/Florence 2021.

ECPAT/INTERPOL/UNICEF, *Disrupting harm in Uganda: Evidence on online child sexual exploitation and abuse*, Bangkok/Lyon/Florence 2021.

ECPAT/INTERPOL/UNICEF, *Disrupting harm in Thailand: Evidence on online child sexual exploitation and abuse*, Bangkok/Lyon/Florence 2022.

ECPAT/INTERPOL/UNICEF, *Disrupting harm in Tanzania: Evidence on online child sexual exploitation and abuse*, Bangkok/Lyon/Florence 2022.

ECPAT/INTERPOL/UNICEF, *Disrupting harm in Ethiopia: Evidence on online child sexual exploitation and abuse*, Bangkok/Lyon/Florence 2022.

ECPAT/INTERPOL/UNICEF, *Disrupting harm in the Philippines: Evidence on online child sexual exploitation and abuse*, Bangkok/Lyon/Florence 2022.

EU, *Proposal for a regulation of the European parliament and of the council laying down rules to prevent and combat child sexual abuse*, 2022/0155(COD) (11 May 2022).

Gallagher, Anne, *Art. 35 Protection against the Abduction, Traffic, and Sale of Children* in: John Tobin (ed.), *The UN Convention on the Rights of the Child: A Commentary*, Oxford 2019.

Gillespie, Alisdair A., *Adolescents, Sexting and Human Rights*, Human Rights Law Review, Vol. 13 (2013).

Gillespie, Alisdair A., *Child Pornography. Law and Policy*, London 2011.

Gillespie, Alisdair A., *Cybercrime. Key Issues and Debates*, Oxon 2019.

Graw Leary, Mary, *Self-Produced Child Pornography: The Appropriate Societal Response to Juvenile Self-Sexual Exploitation*, Virginia Journal of Social Policy and Law, Vol. 15 (2008).

Hague Conference on Private International Law, *A preliminary report on the issues arising from international surrogacy arrangements*, The Hague 2012.

ICMEC, *Cryptocurrency and the trade of online child sexual abuse material*, Virginia 2021.

Internet Watch Foundation, *The Annual Report 2020*, available here: https://www.iwf.org.uk/report/iwf-2020-annual-report-face-facts.

INTERPOL, *Threats and Trends Child Sexual Abuse and Exploitation: COVID-19 Impact*, Lyon 2020.

Ireland-Piper, Danielle, *Extraterritorial Criminal Jurisdiction: Does the Long Arm of the Law Undermine the Rule of Law*, Melbourne Journal of International Law, Vol. 13 (2012).

ITU, *Guidelines on Child Online Protection*, Geneva 2020.

Joining Forces, *Ending Violence against Children and COVID-19*, June 2019.

Kaime, Thoko, *The Foundation of Rights in the African Charter on the Rights and Welfare of the Child: A Historical and Philosophical Account*, African Journal of Legal Studies, Vol. 3 (2009).

Kardefelt-Winther, Daniel / Maternowska, Catherine, *Addressing violence against children online and offline*, Nature Human Behaviour (2019).

Kardefelt-Winther, Daniel/ Day, Emma/ Berman, Gabrielle/ Witting, Sabine K./ Bose, Anjan, *Encryption, Privacy and Children's Right to Protection from Harm*, Office of Research—Innocenti Working Paper, Florence 2020.

Kimberly, Mitchell/Ybarra, Michelle/Korchmaros, Josephine, *Sexual harassment among adolescents of different sexual orientation and gender identities*, Child Abuse and Neglect, Vol. 38 (2014).

Kolossa, Stephan, *The charm of jurisdictions: a modern version of Solomon's judgment?*, Voelkerrechtsblog, 5 June 2019, available at: https://voelkerrechtsblog.org/the-charm-of-jurisdictions-a-modern-version-of-solomons-judgment/ (last accessed: 14 November 2021).

Leiden Universiteit/Waag, *Code for Children's Rights*, Leiden 2021.

Livingstone, Sonia/Bulger, Monica E., *A Global Agenda for Children's Rights in the Digital Era. Recommendations for Developing UNICEF's Research Strategy*, Florence 2013.

Livingstone, Sonia/O'Neill, Brian, *Children's Rights Online. Challenges, Dilemmas and Emerging Directions* in: van der Hof, Simone/van den Berg, Bibi/Schermer, Bart (eds.), *Minding Minors Wandering the Web: Regulating Online Child Safety*, The Hague 2014.

Lumos, *Cycles of exploitation: the links between children's institutions and human trafficking*, London 2021.

Maalla M'jid, Najat, *Report of the Special Rapporteur on the sale of children, child prostitution and child pornography*, A/HRC/25/48 (23 December 2013).

Maalla M'jid, Najat, *Report of the Special Rapporteur on the sale of children, child prostitution and child pornography*, A/HRC/22/54 (24 December 2012).

Maillart, Jean-Baptiste, *The limits of subjective territorial jurisdiction in the context of cybercrime*, ERA Forum 2019.

Manning, Cliff, *A framework for digital resilience: supporting children through an enabling environment*, LSE Blog, 20 January 2021, available here: https://blogs.lse.ac.uk/parenting4digitalfuture/2021/01/20/digital-resilience/ (last accessed: 12 December 2021).

May-Chahal, Corinne/ Palmer, Emma, *Rapid Evidence Assessment. Characteristics and vulnerabilities of victims of online-facilitated child sexual abuse and exploitation*, Lancaster 2018.

Millet, Kate, *Beyond Politics? Children and Sexuality* in: Carole S. Vance (ed.), *Pleasure and Danger. Exploring female sexuality*, Boston 1984.

Mzikenge Chirwa, Danwood, *The merits and demerits of the African Charter on the Rights and Welfare of the Child*, International Journal of Children's Rights, Vol. 10 (2002).

NDR, *Kindesmissbrauch: Warum löscht die Polizei die Bilder nicht?*, 2 December 2021, available here: https://daserste.ndr.de/panorama/archiv/2021/Kindesmissbrauch-Warum-loescht-die-Polizei-die-Bilder-nicht,kindesmissbrauch396.html (last accessed: 12 December 2021).

Oerlemans, Jan-Jaap, *Investigating cybercrime*, Amsterdam 2017.

Ost, Suzanne, *A new paradigm of reparation for victims of child pornography*, Legal Studies, Vol. 36 (2016).

Ost, Suzanne, *Criminalising fabricated images of child pornography: a matter of harm or morality?*, Legal Studies, Vol. 30 (2010).

Ost, Suzanne/Gillespie, Alisdair A., *To know or not to know: should crimes regarding photographs of their child sexual abuse be disclosed to now-adult, unknowing victims?*, International Review of Victimology, Vol. 25 (2018).

Osula, Anna-Maria, *Mutual Legal Assistance & Other Mechanisms for Accessing Extraterritorially Located Data*, Masaryk University Journal of Law and Technology, Vol. 9 (2015).

Osula, Anna-Maria, *Transborder access and territorial sovereignty*, Computer Law and Security Review, Vol. 31 (2015).

Palmer, Tink, *Digital dangers. The impact of technology on the sexual abuse and exploitation of children and young people*, Ilford 2015.

Paul, Kari, *OnlyFans ban on sexually explicit content will endanger lives, say US sex workers*, The Guardian (20 August 2021), available here: https://www.theguardian.com/us-news/2021/aug/20/onlyfans-ban-porn-sexually-explicit-content-risk-lives-sex-workers (last accessed: 5 October 2021).

Pullen, Philip J., *Nail in the MLAT Coffin: Examining Alternatives Solutions to the Current Mutual Legal Assistance Treaty Regime in International Cross-Border Data Sharing*, North Carolina Journal of International Law, Vol. 44 (2018).

Ricardo, Christine/ Bake, Gary, *Men, Masculinities, Sexual Exploitation and Sexual Violence. A Literature Review and Call for Action*, Washington 2008.

Ryngaert, Cedric, *Research Handbook on Jurisdiction and Immunities in International Law*, Cheltenham 2015.

Scurry Baehr, Kristina, *Mandatory Minimums Making Minimal Difference: Ten Years of Sentencing Sex Offenders in South Africa*, Yale Journal of Law and Feminism, Vol. 20 (1).

Sherman, Megan, *Sixteen, Sexting, and a Sex Offender: How Advances in Cell Phone Technology Have Led to Teenage Sex Offenders*, Boston University Journal for Science and Technology Law, Vol. 17 (2011).

Singhateh, Mama Fatima, *Impact of coronavirus disease on different manifestations of sale and sexual exploitation of children. Report of the special rapporteur on the sale and*

exploitation of children, including child prostitution, child pornography and other child sexual abuse material, A/HRC/46/31 (22 January 2021).

Singhateh, Mama Fatima, *Report of the Special Rapporteur on the sale and sexual exploitation of children, including child prostitution, child pornography and other child sexual abuse material*, A/75/210 (21 July 2021).

Skelton, Ann/ Mezmur, Benyam, *Technology changing @ a Dizzying Pace: Reflections on Selected Jurisprudence of the UN Committee on the Rights of the Child and Technology*, Peace Human Rights Governance, Vol. 3 (2019).

Sloth-Nielsen, Julia, *The African Charter in the Rights and Welfare of the* Child in Trynie Boezaart (eds.), *Child Law in South Africa*, Johannesburg 2017.

Smahel, David / Subrahmanyam, Kaveri, *Adolescent Sexuality on the Internet: A Developmental Perspective* in: Saleh, Fabian M./ Grudzinskas, Albert J./ Judge, Abigail M., *Adolescent sexual behavior in the digital era*, Oxford 2014.

Suojellaan Lapsia, *CSAM Users in the Dark Web. Protecting Children through Prevention*, Helsinki 2021.

Svantesson, Dan/ Gerry, Felicity, *Access to extraterritorial evidence: The Microsoft cloud case and beyond*, Computer Law and Security Review, Vol. 31 (2015).

Terre des Hommes, *Child Safeguarding Guidance for Journalists*, September 2014.

Titheradge, Noel/Croxford, Rianna, *The children selling explicit videos on OnlyFans*, BBC (27 May 2021), available here: https://www.bbc.com/news/uk-57255983 (last accessed: 5 October 2021).

Tobin, John, *Art 36 Protection against All Other Forms of Exploitation* in Tobin, John (ed.), *The UN Convention on the Rights of the Child: A Commentary*, Oxford 2019.

Tobin, John, *The Optional Protocol on the Sale of Children, Child Prostitution, and Child Pornography* in: Tobin, John (ed.), *The UN Convention on the Rights of the Child: A Commentary*, Oxford 2019.

Tobin, John/ Field, Sarah M., *Art. 16 The Right to Protection of Privacy, Family, Home, Correspondence, Honour and Reputation* in Tobin, John (ed.), *The UN Convention on the Rights of the Child: A Commentary*, Oxford 2019.

Tobin, John/Cashmore, Judy, *Art. 19 The Right to Protection from All Forms of Violence* in: Tobin, John (ed.), *The UN Convention on the Rights of the Child: A Commentary*, Oxford 2019.

Tobin, John/Seow, Florence, *Art. 34 Protection from Sexual Exploitation and Sexual Abuse* in: Tobin, John (ed.), *The UN Convention on the Rights of the Child: A Commentary*, Oxford 2019.

UN Economic and Social Council, *Guidelines on Justice in Matters involving Child Victims and Witnesses of Crime*, E/CN.15/2005/L.2/Ref.1 (25 May 2005).

UN Economic and Social Council, *Question of a draft optional protocol to the Convention on the Rights of the Child on the sale of children, child prostitution and child pornography, as well as the basic measures needed for their eradication*, E/CN.4/1998/103 (24 March 1998).

UN General Assembly, *Declaration on the Inadmissibility of Intervention in the Domestic Affairs of States*, A/RES/36/103 (9 December 1981).

UN General Assembly, *Optional Protocols to the Convention on the Rights of the Child on the Involvement of Children in Armed Conflict and on the Sale of Children, Child Prostitution and Child Pornography*, A/RES/54.263 (25 May 2000).

UN Human Rights Committee, *Tonnen v. Australia*, Communication No. 488/1992, U.N. Doc CCPR/C/50/D/488/1992 (1994).

UN, *Guiding Principles on Business and Human Rights*, New York 2011.

UN, *Policy Brief: The Impact of COVID-19 on children*, New York 2020.

UNICEF East Asia and the Pacific and Young and Resilient Research Centre, *Evaluating Online Safety Initiatives: Building the evidence base on what works to keep children safe online*, Bangkok, 2022.

UNICEF Innocenti, *Handbook on the Optional Protocol on the Sale of Children, Child Prostitution and Child Pornography*, Florence 2009.

UNICEF Innocenti, *The sale and sexual exploitation of children in the context of sport and sporting events*, Florence 2020, p. 1.

UNICEF Innocenti, *The sale and sexual exploitation of children: Migration*, Florence 2020.

UNICEF, *#Reimagine Justice for Children*, New York 2021.

UNICEF, *Access to Justice for Children in the era of COVID-19: Notes from the Field*, New York 2020.

UNICEF, *Action to End Child Sexual Exploitation and Abuse. A Review of the Evidence*, New York 2020.

UNICEF, *Global COVID-19 Final Report*, New York 2021.

UNICEF, *Regulation of Child Online Sexual Abuse. Legal Analysis of International Law & Comparative Legal Analysis*, Windhoek 2016.

UNICEF, *Research on the Sexual Exploitation of Boys: Findings, ethical considerations and methodological challenges*, New York 2020.

UNICEF, *The State of the World's Children 2017*, New York 2017.

United States Sentencing Commission, *Mandatory Minimum Penalties for Sex Offences in the Federal Criminal Justice System*, Washington 2019.

UNODC, *Assessment Toolkit—Trafficking in Persons for the Purpose of Organ Removal*, Vienna 2015.

UNODC, *Comprehensive Study on Cybercrime Draft—February 2013*, New York 2013.

UNODC, *Manual on Mutual Legal Assistance and Extradition*, New York 2021.

UNODC, *Study on the Effects of New Information Technologies on the Abuse of Children*, New York 2015.

US Department of State, *Trafficking in Persons Report 2021*, Washington 2021.

Vandenhole, Wouter/Erdem Türkelli, Gamze/Lembrechts, Sara, *Children's Rights. A Commentary on the Rights of the Child and its Optional Protocol*, Cheltenham 2019.

WeProtect Global Alliance, *Global Threat Assessment 2019*, London 2019.

WeProtect Global Alliance, *Global Threat Assessment 2021*, London 2021.

WeProtect Global Alliance, *The Sexual exploitation and abuse of deaf and disabled children*, available here: https://www.weprotect.org/wp-content/uploads/Intelligence-briefing-2021-The-sexual-exploitation-and-abuse-of-disabled-children.pdf (last accessed: 24 April 2022).

WHO, *INSPIRE—Seven Strategies for Ending Violence against Children*, Geneva 2016.

WHO, *Report of the Consultation on Child Abuse Prevention*, Geneva 1999.

Witting, Sabine K., *Child sexual abuse in the digital era—Rethinking legal frameworks and transnational law enforcement collaboration*, Leiden 2020.

Witting, Sabine K., *Transnational by default: online child sexual abuse respects no borders*, International Journal of Children's Rights, Vol. 29 (2021).

Witting, Sabine K., *Walking a tightrope on an ethernet cable. The CRC Committee's 25th General Comment Children's Rights in relation to the digital environment*, Leiden Law Blog, 2nd April 2021, available here: https://leidenlawblog.nl/articles/walking-a-tightrope-on-an-ethernet-cable (last accessed: 15 October 2021).

Wright, Valerie, *Deterrence in Criminal Justice—Evaluating Certainty vs. Severity of Punishment*, Washington 2010.

Printed in the United States
by Baker & Taylor Publisher Services